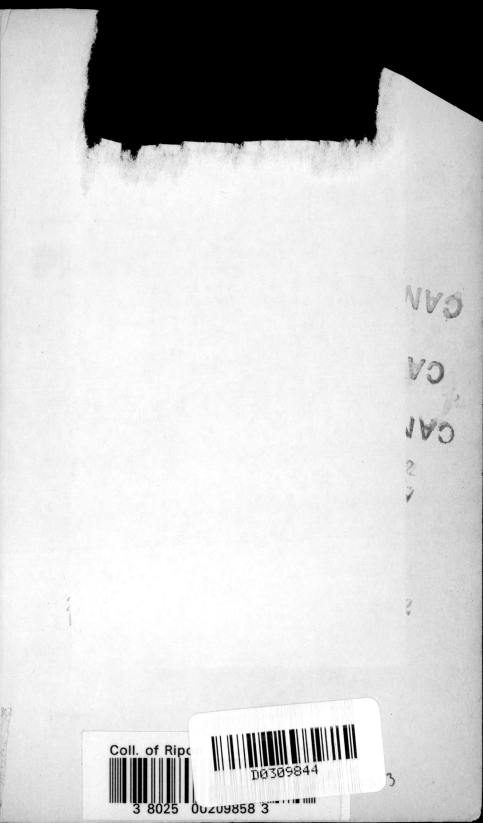

Movement and Dance in the Primary School

MOVEMENT AND DANCE
IN THE
PRIMARY SCHOOL

Now and in the Nineties

Violet R. Bruce

OPEN UNIVERSITY PRESS
Milton Keynes · Philadelphia

Open University Press
Open University Educational Enterprises Limited
12 Cofferidge Close
Stony Stratford
Milton Keynes MK11 1BY

and
242 Cherry Street
Philadelphia, PA 19106, USA

First Published 1988
British Library Cataloguing in Publication Data

Bruce, Violet
Movement and dance in the primary school:
now and in the nineties.
1. Primary schools. Curriculum subjects: Dancing – For teaching
I. Title   372.8'6
ISBN 0–335–09506–2
ISBN 0–335–09505–4 Pbk

Library of Congress Cataloging-in-Publication Data

Bruce, Violet R.
Movement and dance in the primary school:
now and in the nineties / by Violet R. Bruce.
p.   cm.   Includes index.
ISBN 0–335–09506–2.
ISBN 0–335–09505–4 (pbk.)
1. Movement education.   2. Dancing for children – Study
and teaching (Primary)   I. Title.
GV452.B77   1988
372'.216—dc19
Typeset by Scarborough Typesetting Services
Printed in Great Britain by J. W. Arrowsmith Ltd, Bristol

Contents

Foreword

Anyone who has observed healthy young children cannot fail to be immediately struck by their restless natures, their constant urge to move, their need to learn their own physical capabilities. It appears just as fundamental a need to them as play, food and sleep. Movement is one of a child's first means of expression and to neglect to provide for children's physical needs and experiences is to ignore a vast area of development in the early years. On entering primary school, children need to practise and enhance their developing movement skills in a variety of ways and be encouraged to gain mastery over their bodies and quality in their physical expressions. There is probably no better means of achieving this than through creative dance, which provides a unique vehicle for integrating body control and movement quality, both of which lead, in turn, to control of thinking processes. The old adage 'healthy body: healthy mind' has much to commend it.

Yet creative dance, it appears, is not so much in evidence in primary schools today. Much of primary education, as many reports and vast quantities of research have shown, focuses on children's intellectual development, frequently at the expense of emotional, social and physical concerns. Yet my own teacher training in the immediate post-Plowden era reflected a real commitment to active learning and nowhere more so than in the area of dance, an impetus which had been inspired by the work of Rudolf Laban and his followers – one of whom is the present writer, Vi Bruce.

In this book, the author attempts to redress some of the balance by presenting a carefully conceived and well-reasoned argument for the greater inclusion of creative dance in the primary curriculum and the practical means by which this can be achieved. Vi Bruce, herself an exemplary dance teacher, shows within the book how teachers may enhance their own knowledge and skills, and structure creative movement for primary children. The writing is pervaded by her own liveliness and commitment to children's expressive movement skills and qualities, and the many 'hidden' advantages this can ultimately present for young children in terms of learning across and throughout the rest of the curriculum. Her integrative approach will be welcomed by primary teachers as, at last, they will have the opportunity to consider dance as an inherent part of 'normal' classroom practice rather than something which inhibits and interferes with on-going activities. Her book will be even more welcome as so little has been written recently on the subject.

A report, commissioned by the Physical Education Association of Great Britain and Northern Ireland in 1987, comments harshly on the lack of breadth, balance, progression and continuity in all primary physical education and nowhere more so than in creative movement and dance: the problem, it seems, stems from teachers' lack of confidence in this area. I am sure that this book will be welcomed as a new source of inspiration, strength and guidance for primary teachers, whether beginners or those requiring a fresh approach. With the insight provided, and the undoubted enthusiasm and commitment of the children, little encouragement will be needed, I am sure, for teachers to experiment with creative movement as a source of pleasure, enjoyment and learning for themselves and the children alike.

Janet R. Moyles,
Lecturer in Early Years Education,
University of Leicester.

Acknowledgements

To children who have taught me through the years. To readers of the original script for their help and ideas. To Leicester and Leicestershire Heads, teachers and children for their cooperation and photographs. To Mr Butler, Leicester University, for his help with photography. To children whose poetry I have collected at various times, especially to those whom I have been unable to thank individually. To Mrs Janet Moyles for her encouragement at all times and for her Foreword. To Stanley Thornes (Publishers) Limited, Gloucestershire, for permission for *The Coral Island*. To Laura Cecil for and on behalf of The James Reeves Estate for Slowly and Mrs Button. To Dance and the Child International for permission to use 'Dancing Figures' for the cover of this book.

Introduction

It has been some years since I realized how teachers of our children in their early years, from the nursery to entry into senior education, needed more help with teaching movement leading to dance, which involves dramatic, musical, literary, environmental and many other interests. Our primary schools have not, I think, lost their way in the quest for 'up to date' subjects – one enters almost any school for younger children and finds a wonderland of activity, colour and sound which lifts the spirit – but where the education of that most urgent and natural activity loosely called 'movement' is concerned, there is often much confusion. Should it be a semi-structured 'letting out' period? Should it be a technique allied to ballet or contemporary dance, to jazz dance or aerobics because a teacher has encountered such styles? It may perhaps be a simple modification of yoga. All these can be found where teachers are unsure. How then should our movement education have developed and which direction should it take in the immediate future?

Movement played an important part in the fine education which developed in many places in the post-war years for young children. The lively, happy, learning atmosphere is still there, but on the whole the quality of the movement lesson has not been maintained. Why is this? We shall see as we look at the history of movement education during this period that it is probably because a depth of knowledge was never adequately established for most teachers. Understanding needs to be at a level which makes it possible for a teacher to find his or her own way in any new situation, for all children as individuals and as a group. With enough knowledge and understanding teachers would be able to offer relevant learning experiences as our culture changes, as the inner city has special needs, as children's lives are influenced by technological advances, by television, by music groups and all that surrounds them. As it is, many teachers cannot adapt and there is not sufficient re-education or fresh initiative from teacher training.

We have to find a way, with appropriate energy and sincerity, to achieve real quality, for all, to go with our changing culture, without throwing overboard the rich freedom of a young child's imagination, his ability to enter the world of fantasy with and beyond science fiction and rhythmically beyond the incessant beat of 'pop' music. The world as encountered by some of our children is mechanical and frighteningly ugly, but excitement and beauty, influenced by natural harmony, is still relevant. Can we safeguard the balance and preserve many interests while entering the contemporary scene?

We have to bridge the gap between what was thought to be right if it came from the children, which was free, expressive and perhaps creative, and that which has precision, requires increasing bodily skill and coordination and demands movement memory; but just as the former is inaccurate and shallow in its thinking we must beware of unwise adherence to the latter which may well ignore the true development of children. Teaching must consider the very nature of the child. This would be wasted and destroyed if we tried to produce 'clever' dancers before the body, mind and spirit can cope.

So I try to write for the future, with great optimism that teachers will understand the need for knowledge about movement, dance, drama and music. I believe that these practical arts are a vital part of a child's learning and an intimate part of total development, of body and mind, of language and concept, and the ability to concentrate, learn and share. It is, of course, necessary that those who administer, guide and plan resources should realize how essential the arts are in education, and the wealth of their contribution to learning, so that in their anxiety about 'basic' studies they do not legislate artistic subjects out of the curriculum.

Here I pay tribute to the books which have been written and are still available. Much of my text must of necessity be re-statement, but it is important that we coordinate the material anew and look at it with contemporary understanding.

One must pay tribute to Rudolf Laban who contributed so much to our knowledge of the individual and human movement quality, to observation and analysis of movement so that with intelligent understanding we could bring to children a synthesis of learning, exploring, creating and then more learning with clarity and discipline.

One must pay tribute to many devoted teachers and writers who with energy and dedication sought Laban's teaching and have worked through the past decades in schools and colleges, teaching, training teachers and writing.

As one becomes animated and more sure about techniques of movement, and the way in which they should pave the way to composition and choreography, particularly at senior level, one realizes that one should never disregard or take for granted the education of the human body as the instrument, at any age. The task is making the technique right. Certainly body training which is learned rigidly and passed on in the same manner is not right. We are concerned with all children, the thin and wiry, the heavier ones who may move with immense sensitivity but with less agility, those whose movement is less fluent, those who tend to be solitary, those who rejoice in relationship, those who love movement and those for whom it is less welcome. Now we have in our classes children whose movement or comprehension or both may be handicapped, who may have sensory or motor problems. So our teaching needs to allow all children to 'come in', but that does not mean that quality will be poorer. It means that there will be many pathways, much variation in achievement and much sharing of ability. This is where the knowledge which Laban opened up for us is so valuable. Its very analysis allows for the above and ensures the quality which one seeks.

Teachers must know as much as possible about the movement potential of the human body as it develops. There must be much practical teaching, coaching and criticism of the best kind, some repetition and insistence upon what makes for perfection in a movement phrase or composition. In the service of such learning there must be interchange between children and teacher. Many disciplines and areas of knowledge contribute, but one should always be aware of which stage the children have reached, their needs and abilities.

Progression in the arts has been a problem. How can one ensure that it happens for all? There is a chapter devoted to this vexed question. Teachers of young children have constant contact and are in a good position to observe and to assess the needs of the individual child and of the group. Observation is not easy, however. A teacher has many tasks as she stimulates, guides, controls and corrects a group of children which even now may be large in number. So many distractions occur. There are so many individual needs. So when one says 'observe', one is really talking about an ability which can only arise with experience and an analysis of the task. 'Observation in a movement lesson involves watching what the child does in action and in stillness, the quality of the movement, the child's ability to cope with himself, others and the space around. It involves the awareness of attitudes and relationships and the way in which each child responds to the situation. Teachers become more skilful observers than most people. Indeed they must, as their observation must guide the very act of teaching.

Perhaps it is appropriate here to talk a little about the place of men and women, boys and girls in the art of dance. Male teachers bring valuable attributes and balance to the work even though there is in any teacher's dance course a predominance of female teachers. In this country there is to some extent still a male aversion to dance. However, we have television programmes showing contemporary dance, choreographic works by such fine artists as Robert Cohan, Robert North, Paul Taylor and many others, and much which demonstrates vividly the power, excitement and agility of dance. There is much dance activity in arts centres and indeed in many schools. The body can do things which startle, which are daring, which some children will wish to accomplish and to include in their dance. Boys in particular sometimes need to somersault, to balance precariously, to turn cartwheels and to throw themselves in abandon. Obviously these skills must be accomplished safely, and so must be well coached, and ultimately with relevance must become part of the art of dance.

The important thing is that boys and girls, men and women, all contribute their own abilities, their variation of strength, energy, sensitivity and creativity. They must all grow beyond what they can achieve easily. The self-image of every child is important. All play a part. All gain from each experience and from others around them.

No writing will replace the experience of doing, discussing, observing and teaching, but teachers need the written word to help them to retain, to remind and to give confidence as they embark upon an aspect of their work which needs courage, knowledge, belief and the ability to play oneself.

The reader must excuse some repetition in this script. It is inevitable that as one writes about children and about an activity which so embraces their energies, one reiterates characteristics and observations which are relevant to various areas of discussion.

CHAPTER 1

Looking Back Before Looking Forward

It is interesting and illuminating to look back briefly at the beginning of movement and dance in our primary schools.

There was once the need for 'drill' in the fresh air of the yard or playground, incorporating the discipline necessary for the kind of learning of the time. Later came greater care for the body and its education through more pleasurable exercises, with and without small apparatus such as balls, hoops and ropes, and including games activities. Later still, largely through the work of Rudolf Laban came the concern for movement quality, the importance of giving a place to expressiveness and artistry in movement, to children's own inventiveness and so to dance. This process was led and accelerated by the whole attitude towards children's learning. Pioneers in the nineteenth century were such people as Robert Owen, Pestalozzi and Froebal; and there were enthusiasts who continued and expanded such thinking. Certainly, in Britain, nursery and infant schools led the way through the dedication of such teachers as the McMillan sisters, Susan and Nathan Isaacs, Dorothy Gardiner and many others. How could 'drill' exist when such an atmosphere of learning was developing?

Alongside 'drill', which preceded Physical Training and Physical Education, singing games took place in schools where teachers were enthusiastic. Singing games belong, of course, to the street and the playground, and are part of our culture; like whips and tops, hoops and skipping ropes they come and go in and out of fashion. They exist all over the world in the folk ways of children. There were always wise teachers who fostered them, but they did not and do not take the place of movement education. Folk dances, country dances and maypole dances may take place in a particular school or area because a teacher has knowledge and enthusiasm or because there is a tradition. Folk dances belonging to communities from other countries, from Norway, Sweden, France and other parts of Europe, were available in print, were enjoyable and easy to teach. Alongside a kind of drill in my council school in London went 'Greek Dance'; this privilege existed because there was a teacher who loved dance and a Head who could be persuaded that time could be spared from 'basics'.

So, as always, where there was someone who cared enough and made the point clearly enough, children danced as part of state education, otherwise such dance was available in private classes and schools.

All children, of course, danced. Who can stop children from dancing with excitement, with joy, with an overflow of energy, whether it be down the garden path or alley way or along the paving stones? Always children have swirled, twirled and performed the dance, unique to the young child.

Perhaps the visual arts were foremost in the quest for children's expressiveness. Cizec, Viola and so many educators in this country saw further than linear drawing and copying, and opened up the whole area of art in education, of child art. A. R. Stone, a Birmingham headmaster, was one of these. During the war, he saw how valuable the arts were for the children in his school whose surroundings were dismal, whose circumstances were often traumatic and for whom the war meant interrupted nights and time spent in the shelters. He knew that there was necessity for relief, that on many days concentration was bound to be limited, and in his wisdom he turned to the arts to replace for the children some of the lost energy and to lift the spirits. He grasped first drama and art, about which he had knowledge, but realized that something different from country dancing was needed to energize and bring joy in movement. He discovered the work of Diana Jordan, who preceded Laban in this country. She had studied for a time in Europe and had become involved with Laban's teaching, and as early as 1938 she wrote *The Dance as Education*. At the time she was teaching older children in a private school, but she obviously knew even then that children's dance must be concerned with sensory, expressive and creative attitudes. She was, like many pioneers, a genius in her field. She applied her poetic spirit to her teaching. Her belief was absolute, her quest for knowledge eager, and she worked to bring her artistic gifts and understanding to teachers and children in Worcestershire, later in the West Riding and then to many throughout Britain. I speak at some length about Diana Jordan because we are inclined to forget quickly those people who were so inspired, who worked so hard and gave so much to so many in this field. It is possible that of such inspirers Miss Jordan contributed in a major way to dance for young children.

As visual arts continued in our infant and junior schools, drama also became freer, more concerned with children's play, which children themselves enjoy sincerely. Teachers like Arthur Stone and Peter Slade led the way here. Music was much slower and took time to become music-making, which is less hindered by the mechanics of reading the score and less unsympathetic to the fact that young children take time to establish pitch in their voices. Many teachers are afraid of their ability to teach music and we still lack musicality in much of our dance teaching. However, although a little late, much progress has been made in the development of music even in our primary schools. Great is the success of music-making in education in many places. It may soon creep more into the corners of less privileged areas.

Dance received its greatest impetus when Rudolf Laban came to this country as a refugee from Germany. He had strong beliefs as the result of long study and deep knowledge about the nature of human movement and man's need to dance. He was still developing his thinking and his analyses as he was developing his method of notating movement. Here he was, in a new country, soon to be torn by war, with another language to master to express his ideas, and he encountered a nation for whom movement education was in doubt.

The 1933 syllabus was, as it were, the teachers' bible of physical education. Most teachers possessed this precious document whose tables told them the process and content of the P.E. lesson for their weekly class. It was, I think, a good book. It offered ideas in abundance and there were many well-chosen illustrations. There was striving to ensure good quality in the performance of the activities and teachers could feel relatively secure even if many might not observe well and might know too little about the purpose of an exercise. There were in most areas P.E. advisers who went to schools to demonstrate and to help.

Obviously, however, something was about to happen. Rudolf Laban and his colleagues were concerned primarily with dance but such was Laban's approach to movement that there was an obvious link with physical education. The work was welcomed, particularly by the women specialists, as the way physical education might match the educational philosophy which held sway. There are many who have seen this amalgamation as detrimental, who have perhaps misunderstood and often been responsible for delaying the progress of the art of dance in our schools. However, physical education gave a place to movement and dance on the timetable. After all, P.E. was already there, occupying the large space or hall. Whatever one thinks, this acceptance contributed to the rapid embrace of movement education by many who had limited knowledge, but much of the progress took place because the physical education profession, particularly the women, were enthusiastic.

It may well be that the analyses which Laban offered and the ideas which he embraced were grasped too quickly and impatiently. There were a few people who studied avidly, following courses taken by Rudolf Laban himself together with Lisa Ullmann his close colleague, Sylvia Bodmer, Diana Jordan and Joan Goodrich, all pioneers working closely with Laban. Many of these early students of Laban's work went to the Art of Movement Studio in Manchester, later in Addlestone to work continuously for a time. So there came about a nucleus of teachers who gained some depth of knowledge and understanding which must take time, practice and constant re-appraisal. These people, followed by generations of students, continue to teach with varying degrees of wisdom.

Teachers of young children, being caring, searching people, developed much exciting and valuable work in the primary schools. Laban's ideas fitted so well with the ways in which our progressive schools were beginning to work. Many children moved and danced with freedom, absorption and artistry, exploring and creating with great success.

Why then do we seem to have lost so much of this? As our culture perpetually changes, we must be ready to re-appraise, to re-learn, to adapt, observing the children with fresh eyes. Teaching movement and dance in a manner which draws from the children, which develops from what they do, which embraces the contemporary environment and which is concerned for artistry is not easy. A teacher needs to know about the human body, about movement itself, qualitatively and spatially. She needs musical and dramatic knowledge, care, empathy and understanding of what a child is learning about language, ideas and concepts, communication and relationship. She must observe well, be prepared to 'step sideways', to adapt and where possible to help to bring children's work to created form.

Sadly the specialist courses which did provide teachers from some colleges with a good dance background are greatly diminished in number and little dance education is available for teachers of young children generally. However, teaching itself is an art, which the teacher does master. She cannot be expected to be also a specialist dancer, musician and poet. Although she may have limited special knowledge of movement and dance at first, this will develop with the support of all the skill a teacher of young children has, which guides her everyday teaching, in and out of the classroom. With the artistry of the teacher comes a balance between what one gives and what one receives from the children. Just as a child does not have to be a very good dancer in order to create dance, so a teacher of young children can teach without the greater specialist resources of the person who has studied in depth, who may well be without the riches owned by the teacher who relates closely to the children, through many areas of learning, interest, difficulty and success.

Teachers who have not sufficient knowledge about movement and the art of dance, however, have sometimes lost enthusiasm because they cannot perceive a clear framework and purpose for their work. Sometimes it has been replaced by or injected with techniques or adult type movement skills resulting in failure or a premature cleverness which really returns in a modern way to drill. So we must think again, using all that we had, and all that we can learn about the body, movement quality, spatial attitudes, rhythm, movement memory, exploration and creation and the making of dance for and with the children of today.

In a way there is a dance boom. Dance has now its own degrees and its own recognized research. It plays a prominent part on television, in youth activity and community arts. Certainly there is a growth of recognition and much available energy. There are schools, including primary schools, where dance plays an important part in the curriculum. There are festivals and performances where excellent work is evident.

Concern is not for those schools where there are teachers with expertise and enthusiasm, but for the majority of our primary schools where teachers hesitate because there is not knowledge or confidence to encourage them to approach an area of learning which demands discipline and freedom and the flexibility and creativeness which can bring order out of disorder, with artistry, for all young children in their own right. They are not lesser or 'under-done' senior students but have qualities of freshness, involvement and innovation which are special to the young child.

CHAPTER 2

The Needs of the Present Day

He shall do his work playing and play working.

This quotation comes from *Ten Years of Change*, West Riding Report 1953, compiled by Sir Alec Clegg, then Mr Clegg. Sir Alec was an educationalist and pioneer who cared greatly for the arts for children and gave opportunity to many other pioneers in the West Riding of Yorkshire during his long service as education officer.

Yet even children's play can be misused, perhaps misunderstood by the adult enthusiast. It has to be channelled and the attitude of play fostered and used. Teachers themselves need to allow the imagination freedom, to enjoy fantasy, to explore, invent and rejoice in what one achieves. There are hurdles to surmount, seriousness, frustration, absorption, concentration, but also laughter, pleasure and success. Effort is needed to surmount difficulty, and energy to reach the stage of fulfilment or consolidation. This is a process which is repeated throughout life. One works to accomplish the means so that one may play the piece, perform the dance, act the part, or bring the picture to completion. It is true that with the spontaneity of the young child the processes become intermingled and follow one another rapidly, but there will always be the need for the effort and the joy of production. Effort in play itself is pleasurable for the child.

The introduction to this book already approaches some of the special needs of the present day.

Movement is a child's means of exploration and discovery. It is a natural activity, a developing, ready attribute. Our 'civilized' life often hinders such play. There is a limited space, a lack of those environments which invite activity, the climate often encloses and even our care towards children may inhibit them. Dangerous roads, crowded shopping areas, small houses, flats or high rise apartments prohibit freedom of movement. Tightly fitting, snug, warm clothing does not help, but is so often necessary. Some parents and teachers cannot tolerate disturbance in such a close community. Television watching is quieter and safer. We endeavour to remedy this situation with adventure playgrounds and sports facilities, but still we need to be aware of the needs of young children especially to move freely into space, to run and jump, twist and turn, to fall, use the floor, to use power and speed safely, without hindrance and with developing skill.

The bonus available from this natural urge to exert energy is to educate ready movement ability. One encourages its control, its developing coordination and balance, its increasing sensitivity and ability to use speed, to go freely with abandon, to steady with care and to balance the body in stillness. This education gives children the best movement possible for them as individuals, so that they do not face life with decreasing mobility and confidence.

In the years when movement and dance flourished in so many of our primary schools we were so excited by the children's own activity, artistry and joy that we did not foster enough care for the human body. As artistic possibilities grew, the instrument often could not cope at the appropriate level. We were afraid of imposing adult standards upon the child and of 'teaching' him, thereby hindering his own ideas and means of expressing them. This attitude, while fundamentally right, neglected precision, accuracy and clarity. Now we are aware increasingly of a climate which demands achievement, but without enough understanding and the wrong teaching, we strive for performance at the expense of the body and mind. These should be educated to provide the best instrument possible for present and future needs. It is sad to see so many junior children without mobility, resilience and coordination, which should be developed so that by the time they reach the top of the primary school, movement ability is at its height. There is too little 'body education' in school. Apparatus for physical education is explored, which is exciting and excellent if well thought out and presented, but it does not educate the body fully. Games and athletic activities help the acquisition of appropriate skills, but do not replace comprehensive movement training. Where better can this training take place than as a precedent to creative work in the movement or dance lesson, extending in coaching and planning to the whole artistic activity?

It is poor movement education, however, that relies upon tricks and ill-digested imitation, and is limited rhythmically, spatially and qualitatively in order to adhere to what is considered popular. We would not suggest that a picture be painted with messy, poor paint, or that children make do with instruments which make poor sound, so the body must be well tuned for dance. A child's body will not be perfect for every task and we must accept what it can do, allowing exploration, creation and a child's needs to predominate. Creative achievement does not have to wait for bodily perfection. It happens throughout children's experiences and we can strive for perfection.

Just as it is sad to see ill-equipped and poorly moving bodies, it is true that our senses, bombarded as they often are with crude, vulgar form need richer education. We need to awaken awareness of sound, colour, shape, of touch and texture and of the embracing kinaesthetic sense embedded in the body. Primary schools offer an excellent environment and opportunity of appreciation of colour, shape, design and texture. All the senses should be used in abundance. The senses feed experience and the whole world of imagination and reason.

We need the arts at this time so badly. Quite rightly young children should learn about the ever increasing achievements of science and technology. These activities will be exciting and tangible for teachers and children as they master the skills of new machines. Artistic activities are less easily clarified for them and indeed for teachers. Results are less sure. A dance or drama lesson could be an apparent failure, little appears to have been achieved, there is nothing left to show, no measure which can be demonstrated. Just as we tended to become too attached to education which was 'of the child', child-centred and creative, now we might well lose sight of the 'frills' of schooling. Within the arts lies the way to thought, to wisdom, to language which is rich, to relationship and to much that underlies the quality of life.

There is cognitive development, the understanding of concepts like over, under, across, backwards, everyone, together.

The world looks different when the body changes its position. The surroundings change appearance when one is tilted or is upside down. The room has a centre, sides, and the longest way is across from corner to corner. Problems are solved and words and ideas become clear in action. We shall study further the relationship with other areas of learning, with sound and music and with words, but learning goes on all the time as school life abounds in experiences which enter into their dancing, acting, talking and writing. Movement education is basic in the diet of a rich curriculum. It is in the centre of learning because it involves the whole being. Movement and dance must not be lost in our future education. It is interesting to note that H.M.I.'s find that children taught through a broad and rich curriculum performed better in tests on 'basics' than those who had a more limited basic diet. One would hardly be surprised!

In the arts there need not be intense competition. A good teacher can ensure that competition is healthy and that some success is available for all children because the activity offers so many possibilities. We must make sure that there is competition within oneself and that each child strives for the highest standard he can achieve.

Fashion, economics, misfortunes and disasters, influences from afar, and of course progressive thinking, affect all we do. The pity is that we waste so much that is good. So, we should take what was so valuable in past decades with us in our increased learning and changing needs.

The teaching of children of mixed ability is a subject which arises often. The primary school is well used to teaching together children with varying abilities. We have now the integration of many of our children who have 'special needs'. Perhaps the movement and dance lesson can cater more easily than some others, although the need for thought and care must not be minimized. All must take part without encountering undue failure or frustration. The delight for the young child especially is that the art offers opportunity for all kinds of experience and ability. Children often display talents that are not obvious in other work. Movement can be for a child his best accomplishment. The child with many difficulties in reading, in numbers, in responding and relating to others, may well find not only success but a pathway to learning. Certainly here is a place for the less able child, but at the same time take care to observe the more able and the gifted children who learn and clarify as they move, as they create form, dance and use sound and words. These children give so much to others in the sharing situation, they gain so much themselves and they too need opportunity and further stimulation.

Teaching children does not follow a rigidly set plan, although as we shall see planning and forward looking are essential. Differences from school to school, from class to class, from day to day can be marked. So the teacher here is especially creative, adaptable, keenly observant and ready to offer her skill to the needs of the moment. It takes much energy and one hopes that other activities can give a teacher some recovery. There will be progress but it cannot be progress in a straight line, steadily unhindered towards the inevitable goal. No teaching lies in this category, least of all the teaching in primary education. The arts are essentially human, full of surprise and excitement and in good hands infinitely rich.

CHAPTER 3

Dance for Young Children

Children must dance. They must be restless. When they think the body becomes restless and ripples with a variety of movement that helps to keep their muscles in harmony with the mind.[1]

What is dance for young children? It is difficult to label the activity that children endow with dance-like quality. One might say, 'Interesting, joyous, exuberant, like energy overflowing'. One might see it as an easier way to state something than using words. At another time one might say, 'It is like acting through movement only', or, 'It is responding to the rhythm', or simply, 'They dance'. It arises from and gives way to what is done in the classroom, what goes on as festival, season, occasion or television programme. Children ally their dancing with their painting, modelling, acting, writing and talking Perhaps the dance is the most direct of all arts. There need be no intermediary instrument or material, no paint or clay. It may be that as Havelock Ellis said, 'Dancing stands at the head of all the arts that express themselves first in the human person'. As in all artistic activity for young children, there are no barriers and expressive work interlocks.

Folk dance plays a part, be it maypole dancing, English country dance, preserved from the past, Scottish country dance, Irish step dancing, Ukrainian, Polish and many dances which exist here because there are many peoples. Afro-Caribbean dance is exciting and energetic and appeals to many of our young people. Asian communities dance, preserving their culture proudly. Dancers like Wayne Sleep, choreography such as Troy Games, skaters like Torvill and Dean, all inspire and bring interest in dance and acceptance that the body can express itself in its own way. We must be constantly aware of changes, developments and opportunities in our culture so that we can absorb, with the children, new ideas and trends. At the same time we must be keenly aware of the special needs of children as we approach all in our movement and dance lessons. Some Asian children, especially girls, are very shy and need encouragement to move freely. There is often great sensitivity in the upper part of the body but hesitation in stepping and running and in joining in contact with others. They have a great love of story and of dramatic ideas. African children are often very energetic and need to use power and speed safely and purposefully. This is a time for many schools of great richness with a variety of contribution.

We are considering the art of dance, the use of movement in its fullest capacity as an expressive medium. Its style is not pre-conceived or inhibited by any fashion or demand. It will be influenced by many things but most of all by the children themselves. So, over and above all traditional dance activity is dance education, proceeding with all learning, including artistic activity in the centre of primary schooling.

When we think of dance immediately we think of rhythm. This we must do in the fullest sense. Movement has its beginning, its progress and its end; it acquires phrasing. So, one grows from the floor towards the ceiling, reaches the highest point, returning to the floor in a roundabout pathway, to stillness. One runs across the hall, stops suddenly, falls slowly, lies still, then rises up ready to run again. One changes from a loose shape to a very strong shape, holds it and allows it to fall back again. Movement can have a strongly repetitive rhythm. 'Get ready and hit, Get ready and hit'; 'step, step, step, step, run fast and stop'. Phrasing becomes more and more important. Movements are rarely single, but one movement follows another, the important parts of the phrase are understood, the transition from one movement to another is made, with awareness. Movement memory begins to develop. An idea can be repeated, the movement made larger or smaller, stronger or lighter, quicker or slower. Later, the whole of a dance idea is memorized so that the body and mind own it, can perfect it and reproduce it. So rhythm in its full sense involves accents, impulse, dying away, stillness, and brings to clarity the strength, time and flow elements, as well as the shape and form of the movement.

This all takes time, involves sensitive guidance and a patient awareness of where the children are in experience, but the continuity of the flow of movement develops throughout the early stages. Rhythm is not pulse, although a pulsating beat may be an element of rhythm, but the flow of the movement through its phrases, sentences and its whole 'story'.

Young children must have the opportunity to move with their own rhythms. Left freely to step, run, stretch, turn, to dance a movement phrase, children will move with differing qualities, speeds and transitions. Gradually children come to manage their movement so that they can respond, if required, to outside rhythm, to a drum beat, to the impulse and lingering sound of a cymbal, to simple music rhythms, to the rhythm of a partner or a group. This ability does come to individual children and to groups of children at differing times and varies very much from school to school. It would often seem to depend upon the richness of the teaching of music and dance. Certainly it varies with cultures. Children in Bali, carried as they are from babyhood to festivals and living constantly in the sound of music, seem to be rhythmically aware at an early age. We must expect great variation and pursue the relationship between movement and an outside rhythm persistently but not rigorously, because the delay is not so important after all and over emphasis could destroy freedom and initiative.

So, dance may arise from an imaginative idea, from a story, a song or music, from an article from the dressing-up box, or from a movement idea itself. It may be the dance of each individual, of two or three, of a group or the whole class may work together. This as we shall see is associated with the process of development which advances so rapidly and often so clearly.

Quite complex dances and dance dramas become possible at the junior stage and children, having achieved created form, do love to repeat and repeat. An old friend of mine, A. R. Stone, who had great experience and wisdom would say, 'Once it does not change at all, throw it away'. This I think has truth. When the dance becomes 'dead', it is time to move on.

There may be no definite moment when the dance art is happening for all and adults may sometimes find it hard to appreciate the art of the child. What is sure is that children become involved with what they are doing, that it takes their concentration, signifies their experience, enhances their whole being and is endowed with quality.

In the past we have placed great accent upon the importance of children creating, upon allowing them to find the whole way. If the artist-teacher inspiration is rich, child centredness happens and artistry is infectious. Most teachers and children, however, need help. Much must come from the teacher. She must deliberately educate the body, enrich the word language, offer ideas, shape the dance for them often and know when she can pass the responsibility to the children, and when she must gently interfere. She will teach, observe, listen, discuss and allow freedom for exploration and creation to take place, but there must be some direction, correction sometimes, and persuasion, as well as permission for the children to find their own way. This is not to suggest that the dance can be unchildlike, only that children need to be taught and guided, the shape of the lesson and progression ensured whenever possible. Freedom cannot be advantageous without security.

Exploration may simply be a 'trying out'. It may be destined to arrive at a conclusion; there will be decision, practice and a coming to creation, in which case there may arise the greatest perfection possible at this stage.

At the present time there is a tendency to accent what is produced. Much influence comes from the media, from competitiveness and adult pressure. This is in contrast to the past when young children performing was almost 'sinful', when creativeness did not have its obvious destination in the arriving at creation and at showing this. The process of learning is indeed valuable for itself and for what it gathers as it proceeds, the bonuses and off-shoots, and the clarification and enrichment of the children's world. The product is important as it consolidates and satisfies the process, bringing landmarks, created form and what is achieved and, for the moment, finalized. Dance is a passing art. It disappears from sight leaving the experience and all that has been gained from the doing.

It is important that children perform, that they share their work, that they discuss it, improve it, that they watch others and learn to criticize well. Performances are occasions when all come to share with the children; so let us have performances, within

the class, for assembly, for parents and other adults, for a festival,
making highlights during the term. The arts look forward; they
are balancers of the curriculum, bringing work to a climax, giving
confidence and pride, contributing to the art form. They help
others to understand and to appreciate, giving pleasure.

Children may well see dance at adult level. Groups from
schools and colleges, from arts centres and theatre come to dance
and perhaps to teach. Often such performances are explained by
the performers, helping the children to understand this more
sophisticated form of their art. We must have knowledgeable and
able visiting groups who are devoted to contributing to the
children's experience and pleasure. Festivals, theatre, films help
to bring the children's dance into place with what is happening
around them. Their work is not something done in isolation in
the primary school: it contributes to the whole and plays its part.
Here we need the sensitive artist teacher who may choose the
work which the children are shown, but who in any case can help
to fill in gaps, to adjust and put the work into perspective and to
integrate the experience.

It is important again to speak of children with varying ability.
As the integration of some of our special children takes place
there is yet more variation in movement ability, in the understanding of words and concepts, in the ease of relationship and in
imaginative energy. At the same time it is increasingly obvious
that children have gifts of various kinds and the movement
opportunity often reveals the ability of those for whom the
classroom offers little success. Here is a chance for some of these
children to shine. The children who succeed, who lead and offer
ideas and solutions are most often those who succeed in many
areas. But it is good that all can share so easily in this activity
where success is so contagious. A teacher must be aware of the
problems if there is physical disability, language poverty or
emotional difficulty, and must be inventive, observant and
patient to give place to all children, to ensure progress for all. It is
just as important to see that the able children have scope as it is to
be positive about those who have difficulties. This is not an easy
task. It means that the work must have flexibility yet it must
remain demanding, interesting and stimulating for all. Mo-
tivation must be there. For the less able there must be the urge to
make effort, for the able the urge must be constantly stimulated.

Reference

1 Rabindraneth Tagore. Part of a conversation quoted by Leonard Elmhirst.

CHAPTER 4

Training the Body with Care

As we see the quite natural popularity of acrobatic-like activity in some gymnastics and dance and the competition which arises, it is important that we discuss training the body as it affects the young child in particular.

Sadly we see in the main young adult population ligaments and tendons which already have lost normal flexibility. The body of the young child is very mobile although it lacks in the early stages the coordination of muscular action which controls movement in joints. We must maintain flexibility alongside growing strength and control, so that the body grows with its optimum mobility. There is no wisdom in over mobility, especially when it is attained and maintained by passive stretching. One must recognize than when body weight is used to persuade mobility as when the legs slide to full abduction using gravity this is passive stretching just as when an outside person stretches the leg. There is nothing wrong with full mobility. What is important is that children have differing structures, varying lengths of long bones, varying muscle lengths and varying potential where mobility is concerned. They may be destined to be stocky with short muscles and a firmly knitted body; they may be destined to have long, slender limbs and perhaps a more mobile body. Most children will grow into something between these extremes. One must urge young children to the fullest movement span so that all joints explore their range, but strength goes alongside mobility and no mobility must be attained to the detriment of other structures.

A young child of three, four or five will lack resilience in running and jumping and one expects their locomotion to be 'flat'. Gradually with encouragement, the bounciness and flexibility of the feet, ankles and knees will develop and the mobility which is so important will be allied with power. The spine is capable of extension but also of flexion and of movement in all directions, so one stretches and curls, bends and twists, using the sides of the body equally. Hip joints allow movement in all directions as do shoulder joints, so one encourages the maximum in stepping and reaching. Mobility is guarded, controlled and limited by muscles and ligaments which surround joints, so we try to ensure the fullest use of the body, maintaining the balance of mobility and strength as nature intended.

Young children use the body as a whole most of the time, isolation of parts coming later. Control of body mobility and the coordination which maintains good posture and optimum movement depend upon muscle tone and growing kinaesthetic awareness. Most young children naturally develop muscle power and grow strong with muscles balancing one another, so that flexors harmonize with extensors, and all muscles of the body work in coordination with one another, in action and relaxation. So, in movement lessons one is concerned with muscle power throughout its range, from greatest strength to the finest, delicate application of energy and to full relaxation. Young children run, jump and leap, push and pull, punch and hit, twist and turn, run and fall, with great energy. From early years movements join together. 'We run and stop, stretch and fall down', 'We grow as tall as we can and then curl back into the floor'. Gradually phrases of movement become more complex, transitions take place, movement passes in accent from one part of the body to another, directions, quality, and the shape of the body change.

Balance of the body develops so that from being planted firmly on widely placed feet the body can balance on one foot, on the balls of the feet, then on the ball of one foot, however fleetingly. Increasing flexibility with control enables the body to balance on many parts, on feet, on feet and hands, on the back or front, on the seat or knees, to change the balance and to venture and explore as children love to do.

By the top of the junior school, at about eleven years, children can be bodily coordinated and skilled. This can break down temporarily as the shape and balance of the body changes in puberty. Much could be said about the kind of training which brings young gymnasts to a high level of acrobatic skill, but they illustrate the coordinated power and mobility which is made possible for the junior body.

The education of the body goes on throughout movement, dance, gymnastics, games, swimming, and indeed during the whole of an active school day. In the movement and dance lesson, however, it is direct, immediate and understood. Much body training goes on in the first part of a lesson, during 'warm up' and preparation, but it continues into the theme of the lesson, giving way to the artistic, creative and imaginative work when it may well be that thoughts and accents upon the body as an instrument become less important.

This necessitates that a teacher understands, observes well, corrects when appropriate and plans intelligently. The education of body movement develops from that which is play. A teacher of young children is expert at positive play. Later, in the junior school, the work becomes more formal, children becoming more knowledgeable about what they are striving to attain in their bodily movement.

It is excellent if a teacher moves well, although she may rarely demonstrate completely. The natural movement quality of teacher rubs off in an uncanny way onto the children's own movement. However, a teacher who feels that good movement has passed her by need not despair. One often says, 'I cannot do this well but you can'. I do not think that a teacher should inhibit her own movement lest children copy her adult movement pattern, but should teach naturally, in mobility and in stillness. Her attention is upon what the children do. All teachers will communicate in their own way. One thing is certain. If the children have been given freedom of choice that is as it should be.

We hear much these days of technique. What is this for young children? For the professional dancer it may be balletic or contemporary in style. Sometimes a technique has supported dancers through the years as has the classical ballet technique. Even this historically secure 'language' varies somewhat, adhering to particular details which have been implanted by a great teacher. Martha Graham in America established a technique which is still the basis for much contemporary dance.

Technique in dance prepares the dancer. It educates the body in a particular way and provides movement patterns which have been or will be used in choreography. At its worst, technique loses sight of its purpose and becomes ill-understood drill. At its best, it is caring, intelligent and progressive, taught with concern for quality, accuracy, rhythm and flow, with care for the individual bodies which are to be the instruments of the dance.

We are speaking here of young children, of mixed ability, with varying physiques, for whom our concern is education in its widest sense. There must be the education of the body-mind relationship which makes it possible for artistic, creative work to be accomplished at all levels, with the use of the rich imagination which, if fed appropriately, is the prerogative of all children.

If the instrument is not in tune and alive with readiness there is frustration, dullness and limitation, just as frustration and failure result from painting with poor colour or modelling with clay which is too wet or too hard.

One might ask, 'When does training the body and its movement become dance?' Perhaps one should offer no universal criteria but look to rhythmic quality, transition, composition and most of all to the flow of movement as it becomes one with the dancer.

Writing as I proceed to do in a somewhat artificially analytical way about the body, movement quality, spatial awareness, rhythm, movement memory and many areas of education and learning which constitute dance, it is important to emphasize that these interlock and are indeed each part of the other. It is artificial to divide them, but necessary in order to enhance the depth of understanding. However, it will be impossible to write with clear division between aspects. Human movement always involves the body, the instrument; aspects of time and energy; it uses space in some way, involves the changing shape of the body and contains the intimate content of the flow which is the essence of human movement.

A teacher of young children cannot be an expert in human anatomy and physiology, but must have a working intelligence of the young body's capabilities, of its development and of what is likely to harm or to establish bad habits. Work must allow for individuality and must be endowed with the kind of freedom which ensures that everyone is involved with safety but with the opportunity to use their potential. Children do not usually bring harm to themselves without undue pressure, even if they have a handicap. It is essential to encourage maximum effort within this concern for individuality.

Among our children there may be future champions whose potential may become obvious and who will enter programmes of special training. Such is the nature of contemporary competition that young children for whom there is aspiration must so soon enter the world of intense, specialized and competitive work. If we are to produce future world class gymnasts, swimmers and games players it seems such sacrifices must be made. Children who are to become professional musicians and dancers must also begin their specialized training very early and one has to make exceptions for all these as we set out to train children's bodies with care for their normal development.

We are aware of circulation and respiration. Most lessons will be balanced in degrees of activity. There will be times when children may well become breathless, times when they are 'sweating'. Then there must be time for ease as breathing steadies and teacher encourages expiration to allow air to enter the lungs steadily, and as pulse rates return to normal. Dance must stimulate energy, pushing the body sometimes to its individual maximum effort. It must be sometimes the educator of ease, delicacy and relaxation.

Important in every lesson is the concern for poise and good posture. This is the use of the body in the best possible manner whatever its activity, but it is brought to awareness by the way in which children stand or walk, the shoulders relaxed, the head lifted from the crown, tall and important.

So for all we must ensure bodily relaxation so that tendons and muscles are capable of releasing tension. We must encourage maximum mobility of all joints in stretching, contracting, turning and wriggling in all possible directions. We must help children to develop strength in activity, ensure increasingly the ability to run, leap, jump and land well, train balance and coordination, together with movement memory, and have constant regard for the developing efficiency of the growing human body.

CHAPTER 5

Body Awareness

Normally, young children quickly become aware of parts of the body, especially of those parts which they can see and whose function is part of early expression and need. Hands manipulate things, they grasp and let go, the face creases and spreads, the legs kick and very soon feet find their way to the floor. They become aware of arms and legs, of elbows and knees. The middle of the body is for a time a base for all the rest and one expects the body to move in bulk. Awareness of the arms, of the ability to stretch into space, to embrace and to make gestures comes about quickly. By the time we are teaching small children about movement they balance in the upright position even though there is a love of the security of the floor.

Body awareness proceeds as parts of the body become important, the hands to stretch and curl, fingers to poke, the head to nod and turn, the elbows and knees to stick out, feet and legs to kick into the air and then to take steps and jumps. One can spin on one's bottom, slide on one's front or back, and roll over and over along the floor. This body knowledge extends as part of movement language and helps the kinaesthetic sense to develop.

As movement ability, creativeness and artistry grow a child becomes sensitive to the parts of the body involved, where the movement begins, passes through and ends. He becomes aware of the particular abilities of the different parts of the body, and by seven or eight years to more detailed awareness of the centre of the body, to the hips, chest and shoulders, to the front, back and sides. This development of ability, understanding and sensitivity is not, of course, a uniform one. There is variation from one child

Figure 1   Our big, wide-open hands

to another, between cultures and locations. Handicapped children, for varying reasons, often have difficulty in knowing and ᵗ𝒔ℰ𝒩
isolating parts of the body and this aspect of movement education
is very important indeed for them.

For most children body awareness becomes a natural part of
their movement and dance vocabulary and a requisite for the
coordination, phrasing and flow of one gesture to another, and of
gestures and steps as they combine. So, one can refer to those
parts which begin the movement, those which are most important, those which send the impulse on or which command the
shape of the body in movement and in stillness. Continually one
pays attention to the body and its coordination of parts, as a leg
raised or limbs outstretched help the delicate balance, as the
centre of the body contracts or expands, as the centre of gravity of
the body is changed in space, as the whole body responds
harmoniously or as parts disagree' with the rest. One might
gently touch a body part in passing, encouraging its definition,
opening the fingers, accentuating an elbow, encouraging the
curve in the spine. In this area lies the future perfection of
movement, the keen awareness and kinaesthetic sense in the
whole body, whether moving or still. In running, jumping and
leaping the top part of the body may simply be carried, or the legs

and feet may be still in support as the main movement is in the upper part of the body. The whole body may be moving or parts may be still, but the whole bodily awareness is awake. The head as the extension of the spine completes a movement.

Warming up or 'oiling up' as children often call it, at the beginning of a lesson, very well involves the awakening of the parts of the body. Children will name them as they move; hands, feet, elbows, knees, shoulders, hips, head and the important middle of the body. With young children, playing with shapes as 'statues' brings strongly and with concentration the awareness of body parts, their position and action. Preparing the body for dance does not mean only quick, vigorous activity. It will often mean soft, sensitive stretching, curling, twisting and urging into full range. It is good sometimes to use the floor so that balance is not a problem, to find the easy and more difficult ways of moving and where parts of the body will go.

Very soon, of course, the body is concentrated upon its wholeness. Young children most naturally use large movements where the whole body is involved and one should not over emphasize isolation of parts. It is much more a concentration upon a part than an isolation. Indeed many children who have a physical handicap or who are less progressed than their fellows find the isolation of parts of the body very difficult and too frustrating to tolerate. However, the idea of knowing the body and of sensing its structure, as well as naming it, is important from the beginning. The body is a very personal possession, very important to a child, to his individuality and to his ego.

As one moves one can be acutely aware of one's body, of the way in which feet touch the ground, of the importance of the head, the acuteness of vision as one proceeds along a path, of air around one's limbs as they reach out into space. One listens to one's own breathing in stillness and in motion. At the end of a lesson it is good that children quietly become aware of themselves, lying, easy and still, or standing with poise and pride.

CHAPTER 6

Teaching Movement Quality

One sees and encourages the development of natural actions, stretching, curling, twisting and turning, running, jumping and attaining locomotion and elevation in varieties of ways. So many movement combinations quickly become possible for the young child, but what is so often not observed or taught is quality, which in its variation is the essence of movement. So many techniques are taught without regard to the way in which the movement takes place. Quality makes movement alive, belonging uniquely to the individual. The child is not a mechanically moving object. The quality of the movement relates to life itself, to our constant fighting and indulging, to our resisting and giving way.

Movement, however stimulated, has some measure of power. This will range from the strongest action or position when muscles are tense and hard, to the finest, lightest touch when muscles control with a delicate tension. There may be a giving up of energy and the body becomes soft, floppy and relaxed. With young children extremes are most easily experienced so that they become very strong in stillness, the body hard all over, or they fall into the floor, very soft and floppy. Later there can be degrees of strength as one steps strongly, strikes out or stretches with power. The greatest strength brings about stillness in the body, one is rooted to the ground. The greatest relaxation also brings about stillness, the body loose, soft and seemingly lifeless. Young children enjoy moving strongly, exerting all their strength, pushing, dragging, stretching, curling in tightly, punching, leaping, making themselves into the strongest statue

Figure 2   Jonathan's strength. He really grips the floor and has a wide, firm base.

Figure 3   James' strength

with clear shape. Many children, in their effort, reach a stage of strength which trembles and their faces, gripped in tension, go red as the breath is held. So, quite quickly, the experience having been attained, release must take place. One shakes it away or lets all the tension go in sinking to the floor or changing to a mobile movement.

Extreme lightness often seems to teachers to be a difficult quality for children to experience. In fact their movement can have a delicacy and beauty which takes one's breath. Words describing lightness may be a problem and it is often good to use at first imaginative ideas so that the lightness can come to consciousness. 'Make no sound.' 'I shall not hear you.' 'Go into the air, I still shall not hear you.' 'You are like a balloon going through the air.' It is relatively easy for a child to have careful, delicate fingers or soft, creeping feet, but for the whole body to acquire lightness which lifts it with little tension is more difficult.

As movement arises in variation the quality will exist between extremes and will arise quite naturally as the concentration is upon other things.

Children love the floor and enjoy falling into it. So one can pass from extreme tension to extreme relaxation, from as near to the ceiling as possible, to the floor, first slowly, giving way, then with more confidence. This is a good way to end a lesson sometimes, to bring activity to rest, to quiet, to stillness, to breathing deeply, ready for the next activity, perhaps to meet another teacher.

> Time is the movement of everything that happens. We are spoiled by the mechanical measurement of time.[1]

Whenever we move there is a degree of time. We dart, gesture with suddenness, shiver, shake, thrust, hit, poke, run, stop and start. We feel excited, there is not enough time and we must hurry. With more difficulty for most young children movement can be smooth, sustained, calm, not jerking or hurrying, but taking time as when we stroke an animal friend, smooth our hair carefully or balance along the wall. Movement is not only slow but is held back in sustainment because the time is used with care and purpose.

Going quickly, making very sudden movement, changing one's statue shape so quickly that teacher will not see it happen, all are fun for young children. They are excited, the adrenalin flows, maybe the room comes alive with sound and the stop must be clear and controlled. Going with sustainment may be supported by teacher's voice or by a long sound from a cymbal or gong. Always, of course, there will be accompanying degrees of strength or lightness, so one can push with strength and great steadiness, one goes very quickly across the hall with great lightness.

The time element of movement can change. Slowing movement is quite difficult as the movement is gradually held back until sustainment is reached. From slow to quick is more easily done, 'We start slowly, smoothly, we are getting quicker, quicker, quicker, now very quick, to stop. Sometimes a movement starts suddenly, impulsively, and then dies away as when we make a slashing or whipping action. Sometimes it builds up in speed and comes to an abrupt end as when one traces a firm number 1 from high up to end on the floor.

Quality in movement establishes a two-way pathway. One moves with strength and the sensation in the body arises from that movement. One feels strong or aggressive and the movement emerges expressing the feeling. One is affected by one's movement and conversely one's feelings influence movement. So, in a lesson, what we do can excite or calm, but also we observe children's mood as they rush on a windy day or as excitement rises before a holiday or a special event. One observes lethargy or the healthy quiet of a child as it is visible in posture and gesture.

If one pursues the idea of 'indulging' and 'fighting' in our attitude to movement, one finds that it invades the way in which we use space. Very young children need time and security before they will move freely and happily all over a large space. They tend to stay close to teacher and to one another. One plays with ways of encouraging them to go across the space and eventually to go all over the space, in and out of one another, around and about, without a need to go directly to this end or that or back to teacher wherever she may be. It also takes time before children use the body more fully in space. They need help with the direction. 'To the ceiling.' 'To the floor.' 'Out to the walls.' 'Towards me.' We find ways of helping children to move the limbs further into space and to extend the whole body into the air around them.

Very early one finds the developing awareness of shape. The

body can change its shape, become round like an orange, tall and thin like a lamppost, spiky like a scarecrow or an old, dead tree. This statue game develops as one changes from round, to tall, to twisted, to wide, slowly or suddenly. Body awareness is enhanced, each part of the body is important in relation to another. Care is taken as the shape is formed or released.

Early on one can teach awareness of the shape of the pathway we follow in the large space. We go straight up the hall, around in a ring, right round the edge, we go all over the hall, curving and twisting. What pattern does our pathway make?

A little later one can enter the area of air pathways. We shoot straight up, we draw our initial very large in the air. Gradually the body becomes, as it were, released into space, arms, head and then legs emerging from the centre. The art of dance is reliant upon the movement of the body in the personal space which surrounds it and into the larger space of the hall which is shared with everyone else. One sees in classical ballet very clearly the limbs reaching to the periphery of the body's space from a strong centre. In Indian classical dance the hands, head and face are important and one is especially conscious of the upper space around the body. In contemporary dance the centre of the body is often very strong and mobile and spatial possibilities are explored to their human limit. Folk dances in Europe often use locomotion and the space of the dance area for the patterns and formations. Dance is concerned with space. Kinaesthetic awareness is enhanced as a child increasingly explores and achieves spatial aspirations. Movement is involved with the meaningfulness of being high, or wide, or closed in; of going forward or backward; of circling, surrounding or penetrating through a space. The flow of the movement through space, the rhythm of the movement, its changing direction and quality feed the drama of the dance.

Young children like at first to be safe and steady, the centre of gravity in their bodies firmly over the base as when they move with firm, widely spaced feet. They feel safe near or on the floor. As they become bolder they will play off balance, enjoying a more fragile base such as on one leg, leaning forward or sideways or balancing on the balls of the feet. This leads to toppling and having to manage their weight in a more exciting way. They become able not only to risk being off balance but to manage the recovery as the body moves more often in a more freely mobile fashion. So movement goes from the stability of that which is on balance, safe, sure, to that which is off balance, passing through the air to a more distant security.

Movement may be symmetric as each side of the body balances in the same shape, giving security, but asymmetry arises all the time, increasingly leading to more fluent movement with a greater freedom of flow.

Quality in time, energy, space and flow exists all the time. Sometimes an aspect of quality will become accentuated and may be the theme of a lesson, but always there will be balance because other aspects inevitably come in. This direct concentration upon the way in which one moves, upon how an action is performed is perhaps what characterizes this kind of teaching. It is concerned with the uniqueness of each person and the potential of each to grow beyond what comes most easily. This is a valuable training for all movement, be it artistic or essentially skilful. This is not to say that the pattern of a sequence, a dance step or skill does not itself have to be practised and mastered, but that the rich education of the qualitative range of human movement is of value for all, especially for the dance, if it is to involve the exploration and creativeness of children, as we wish it to do.

As we shall see these aspects of learning are allied all the time with the meaningfulness of words, concepts and ideas. All is brought to awareness together with language and understanding.

Reference

1 Gabo, N. (1962) *Of Divers Arts*, Faber and Faber, London.

CHAPTER 7

Relationships

It is important when discussing basic material and the parts of the syllabus for young children to consider the relationship of teacher with children, of the children to the space around and of one child to another as it develops during the primary years. The interest and vitality of dance becomes enhanced as inter-relationship takes place, as one incites, influences or responds, leads or follows, touches or releases.

At nursery age and often much later, children remain essentially individual. They follow, keeping close together, but respond as individuals. Later, at about seven years, partner relationship begins to be of a positive kind, but it is quite surprising how much this varies. For some children the sharing of ideas with another is a much later concern. A teacher will be able to discern when she has ventured into directed partner relationship too soon. Some confusion and lack of caring for the partner make this obvious. There is concern for all the children, that each has the chance to lead, that each has the task of giving way, that all are involved and that no child is even temporarily left out, and that the task is clearly understood. Working in two's, three's and in groups brings about a new dimension, but it must happen and be developed with a teacher's observation, understanding and honesty about the readiness of the children.

Working in groups comes about at the junior stage. Children's movement ideas begin to relate, moving together, and possible touch bringing excitement and interest in rhythm and shape. Action and reaction, question and answer, shadowing, leading and following, all bring about dance form.

It is important to give time and conscious effort to familiarity and confidence in using the space, often the largest space the children have encountered and very large to the child faced for the first time with a relatively uncluttered area of floor. For a time children stay near to the teacher or even near to the wall, but soon, 'Find a space for yourself' brings response and children quickly become careful of obstacles and danger points. Nevertheless in moments of excitement and intense concentration a teacher must keep an eye open for danger, when for instance she might observe a child preparing to move too near to the corner of the piano, to the window or to another child.

Relationship with the teacher arises naturally and continues from the moment children arrive in the morning. Teachers relate in their own individual ways. Children know a teacher's voice and understand its nuances. They know the words which are used and become used to gestures and a teacher's tempo. Some teachers tend to be among the children, in the midst of them, but aware of all. Some prefer to be 'all-seeing', on the edge of a class. It is important that the teacher can be located and seen whenever necessary. What a compliment it is to a teacher however, when one enters the room and sees only children, deeply involved, the teacher being somewhere amongst them! The personality of a teacher is unique and each finds a way, of encouraging, giving help and praise and inspiring confidence. All children, but especially perhaps those with difficulties, thrive upon the special quiet word or the gentle touch. A teacher praises when there is cause and when there is necessity. She is positive in her coaching but does not praise indiscriminately. Teacher-child relationship in the primary school is most often very close and warm. This is one of the bonuses which arises when most of the day is spent together. Such a relationship means that there is trust. A child does not need to hide failure or difficulty and a teacher can relate to the whole personality of a child as well as joining one area of learning to another.

Relationship comes about between children all the time and in their movement lesson they share the space of the hall and they share ideas. Sometimes they initiate, sometimes they copy, but then the relationship becomes that of working together, in harmony, in antagonism, with and against in the dance sense. They come to accept what others do and begin to learn the true art of criticism.

Figure 4   A partnership with strength.

Figure 5   A partnership with contact.

At junior level groups can work together to explore ideas, to create and to perform. At this stage the task must be well prepared so that the children have the requisite resources and are clear about the nature of their task. They can work in their groups and the teacher has the opportunity to go around to help each group, to talk briefly about ideas and to assist in the process of clarification into movement. It is important that groups are not too large. Five is a good number. More than this may be too large a group, too many ideas are put forth and argument tends to take place. If the class is a large one this will mean that there are many groups, perhaps seven. Inexperienced teachers may find this overwhelming and might prefer to help larger but fewer groups. However, once the teacher and children are involved together and are secure in their project it is possible for a teacher to survey and to deal with a number of groups, giving individual children a greater chance to participate and the created form a greater possibility. It takes time and constant encouragement before children learn to try out ideas quickly. They tend to talk too much. The teacher, as with all exploratory and creative work, will have established a clear framework. This may be tight, the amount of variation allowed being minimal. It may be very large, the task allowing many possibilities and groups may need much time and help. Always, as with all teaching involving creative work, there is the need to balance help and advice with the freedom for the children to make effort, to struggle and to sort out their ideas. Sometimes there will not be success. Groups take differing lengths of time to establish their work and often there will be frustration for those who cannot come to decisions and for those who are waiting impatiently to show their creation. However, a teacher will handle this situation sensitively, using her observation, her knowledge of the children and her ability to use time and opportunity well.

Sometimes groups will present their work only to the teacher, all groups beginning at the same time and resting when finished. Sometimes groups will show their finished work to the others. Group work presents an opportunity to teach the beginnings of observation and the formation and expression of criticism in the most positive way.

Sometimes the group is the whole class and all work together. This may be teacher directed but is likely to be a joint effort, with

Figure 6   A sensitive relationship

some conversation, many suggestions and experiments. Such class creation may prepare for a special occasion. It may be the result of classroom work on a project and much discussion will have taken place. It may simply be that the teacher has perceived the need for all to join together in creative work.

Children's dance experiences then are sometimes individual. This happens naturally in the earliest years but always there will be times when a child will work alone. Then it becomes possible for children to share with others, where there is the drama of interaction, where the shape of movement is enhanced by many contributing. Throughout the primary years a teacher will prepare and teach, giving opportunity for all these relationships to take place, her sensitivity and knowledge ensuring a rich and relevant balance.

CHAPTER 8

The Use of Sound

Teachers are often worried about this aspect of movement education. They feel the need to search for music to accompany all movement which is part of their lesson called dance and one comes to expect at a teachers' course or meeting to be asked for lists of suitable music. One understands and sympathizes with this worry, but the more a teacher learns about movement and the art of dance, the more sure she will be that sound, although closely related to human movement, is sometimes a nuisance to the children and is best used economically.

Let us consider the youngest children. Would sound be stifling and inhibiting to their movement? Do they simply ignore it? Children do need to move as individuals without having always to attempt to conform, with others, to an imposed pattern of sound. See in your mind's eye a four or five year old child, running, hopping, falling, rising and running again. He would ignore the rhythm of music. Young children need to gain coordination and skill without the added task of conforming to an outside rhythm which cannot fit the needs of a class of children who are struggling at their own rate to balance and to manage their movement. Movement does have for an individual its own particular phrasing and flow as does speech, and there is always at any age need for the body to move expressively, sometimes, without sound. This needs and brings about concentration and a deep involvement. There may seem to be less of the kind of pattern emerging which gives adults satisfaction, but it is essential that we think of much of our movement training and the dance which results without imposed sound. The flow of movement is bound up with the act of breathing, with greater and lesser tensions, with spreading into space and closing in from it, with elevation and locomotion, and with relationship. We find that within the silence there comes about for each child a sense of rhythm and phrasing, emerging in time and space from the energy used.

But it is obvious that music excites and fascinates, giving great pleasure to even the youngest children. We have an abundance of music, of beat, rhythm and melody, of the soft, beguiling sound of a guitar, of great orchestras, of the brass band, of drums, of syncopation, of song. Children will move spontaneously or stay still with the body alert as they hear the wonder of musical sound and we would not deny this.

Movement and sound make an exciting combination. Dance and sound have lived together since man danced and dance was probably the first mode of man's expression which found form. We must consider the partnership both ways. Dancers find joy and enhancement in music as accompaniment and as stimulus for their movement, and movement can be a vehicle for the comprehension and appreciation of music, especially for children.

> I am convinced that if a child can capture beauty and nuance
> of feeling in his body, he can grasp that same beauty aurally,
> and in the musical interpretation of making music.

This is what the head of a university music department said as he justified the use of time for his students to dance as a primary concern. Music-making results from movement, as of course does all human expression. There may be the use of the hands in relation to an instrument, the use of the voice, or the conducting of an orchestra when communication is dance-like in character.

We are concerned with the developing, learning child, so we must use these two primary arts, movement and sound, intelligently and with dignity.

Body percussion comes about as one makes movement. The feet beat, tap or stamp the floor. One hears the thrust or the creeping action of the feet as they produce the pattern of locomotion. Fingers make clapping or clicking sounds. Hands make sound on the body. Such body sounds can be delicate as the scurrying of almost silent feet, or they can be firm and hard as when fingers click rhythmically, or they can be heavy and full as the clapping of cupped hands on the thighs.

Vocal sounds, grunts, whistles, breath and mouth noises or singing emerge as children move quite spontaneously. An explosive movement can initiate an explosive sound. A smooth, on-going movement may produce a soft humming. One can encourage sounds of this kind when one knows the children well and all feel free. A teacher may find herself singing her advice to the movers. 'Rise up and up and up . . . sink back, back, back, back, into the floor, and rest.' The spoken words often emerge with the movement rhythm. 'Hit and hit', 'Smoothly and softly', 'Quick, quick, quick.' Words describe in sound and rhythm as well as in meaning the movement as it erupts and progresses.

Using percussion instruments is exciting and rewarding for all. They offer an uncomplicated sound and young children can often already play them; they can be used in the midst of movement as an intimate part, so different from the remote sound of a piano in the corner, or a tape recorder or record player. Here we can have live music. Percussion instruments do need to offer sound of good quality, but even so they are relatively inexpensive, often long lasting and many schools already own good instruments. Tambours, drums, clappers, castanets and other articles can make rhythmic beating or clicking sounds; shakers, rattles, maracas, tambourines, small bells and instruments make shaking sounds; bells, gongs and cymbals make ringing sounds; and xylophones and glockenspiels make melody.

Many instruments can be home made, but we must have 'good' sound. Containers can be filled with a variety of things, stones, beans or peas, which produce different textures of shaking sound. They can be attractive to look at and to hold and can result from the children's own art. They cost little, but must be strong and firm so that the contents do not flow all over the floor.

A teacher may find that she has to handle the tambour, cymbal or gong herself in the early stages. These instruments are large and there may be only one or two available. Soon children will learn to play well and to choose instruments with discrimination. They learn to play a percussion instrument with a sensitive and resilient attitude which brings life to the sound; not sitting, the instrument and body cramped, with no air around both, but

Figure 7   Playing the bells for the others.

mobile, treating the instrument as part of the body. A teacher also needs practice to acquire skill so that sound is full-blooded, sensitive and appropriate. Percussion instruments are not lesser makers of sound. Fingers and hands can be applied with greater versatility: tambours can make strong or soft beating sound. Children can explore, finding the different sounds which can be made near the edge of the skin or in the middle. Gongs and cymbals need to be held away from the body so that they move when struck.

So, percussive sound can stimulate movement, offering beat, rhythm, long, lingering sound, phrasing and variation in quality. Or the player might sensitively accompany children as they move, watching and adapting. The instruments might be played by the dancers themselves. One can move with a tambour or tambourine, even with a gong, and one is mobile with clappers and bells. Or one can use percussion instruments to make accompaniment. One might say, 'I will play for you', or 'If your group decides that sound would help your idea, go to the platform and choose your instrument'. It may be that the sound is the stimulus, it may be accompaniment, or it may be the two are spontaneously merging.

Now to sound that has melody and harmony. Possibilities are great and increase rapidly as one hears yet another kind of sound which excites or interests, which has qualities of simplicity, rhythm or dramatic intensity.

There is the piano, and there may be an accompanist, but frankly unless one is privileged enough to have the services of a creative musician who has knowledge of and much sympathy with movement needs, enjoys the relationship with movement and is often willing to accompany rather than initiate, it is better that one does not have a pianist sitting at the side, waiting rather impatiently to play. One does not need the constant partnership of sound because there must be time for preparation and exploration, times when full concentration must be upon the movement, when the kinaesthetic sense must be acute and when sound might be distraction. Often a pianist is limited to written music which may not have a relationship with the movement. We must consider also the needs of the pianist whose great love is to make music. So, although there are very good pianists who understand movement and give great support and pleasure, it is in most schools necessary for teachers to use many different sounds.

Sometimes a teacher or the children themselves play simple, portable instruments such as recorders. One often finds musical talent among teachers which can sometimes be used in an exciting way.

With a record player or tape recorder there is a wealth of sound electronic, folk song and dance, the music of individual instruments and the full orchestra or group. However, there is also an interruption in the flow of the lesson as the instrument must be put on or off, the disc removed or the tape rewound. A teacher must be as prepared as is possible to avoid interruption and loss of concentration. This is another reason why music should be kept to a minimum in most lessons. It then takes its place, so that there is a special moment when music joins in.

Let us consider 'warm up' music. When one prepares oneself for movement, for dance, it is necessary to awaken the body, to 'oil it up', to warm it perhaps, but mainly to effect the transition from the previous activity, to enliven the senses, to accustom oneself to the larger space and to the others who share it. It is wise to do this at first without sound, concentration is sure, the teacher talks softly as the body shakes, wriggles, stretches, part by part and as a whole, and as the children begin to step, travel and jump. Then this preparation can come to a joyous conclusion with sound which enlivens, with, perhaps, a communal rhythm which encourages movement about the hall. Such music may have continuous pulse. It may be 'pop' music, familiar to the children, music for folk dance used freely, indeed any music which is simple, continuous, unchanging in rhythm and tempo and suitable in time and quality for the children's movement as they go all over the hall. Such 'warm up' music is not essential, but can make a bridge into the theme or themes of the lesson, to bring light into the eye and energy invoked by pleasure to the body, and of course it begins to encourage the coordination of movement with an outside sound. Much freedom can be given here, using such frameworks as, 'Finish your warming up with the music', 'Travel all over the room to the music', 'Use all the space'. Many children will move in a way which seems to ignore the music. One must wait with the understanding of the nursery teacher who waits even for children to leave the security of the wall at the side to join in with the rest.

It would seem to be appropriate here to talk a little about the voice. Here is the intimate instrument, part of the expression of movement in the human body, available to all. Many teachers are embarrassed about using their voices unless they speak words. Children use their voices more freely and without inhibition and will make grunts and hisses, will hum and sing. It is a wise teacher who allows herself to use vocal sound to help rhythm, phrasing and quality. Many teachers have singing ability which could often stimulate or accompany. In any case the voice is very important as it communicates so much in all teaching and tells the children about movement so expressively.

Now we come to music which might be the stimulus for dance

studies or which partners and enhances studies already explored. Ideally there should be mutual creation, musicians and dancers working together. This is rarely possible even at the highest level of choregraphy. In our case it is rarely possible except where, as we have discussed, we use the voice or easily handled percussion instruments. Nevertheless there is a wealth of simple music which can partner movement and dance.

When searching for music one must consider the quality which one needs. Do we need something with vigour and power, should it be delicate, fine in touch, should it be fast, or calm and sustained? Which of these qualities is most important? We may have to sacrifice some of our needs for the most important ones. It is useful to have understanding of descriptive terms used in music, forte, piano, staccato, legato, largo, moderato, presto, although one might only rarely be using the written score. These terms so often describe also the quality of the movement. We most often must come to terms with less sharply defined quality than we would wish. Movement in young children often emerges in extremes of strength or lightness, of quickness, of exuberance or control. Musical composition does not often produce this in the required simplicity. One might want music which is extremely powerful but find only music which is moderately strong. This brings about the need for the children to explore greater and lesser strength. Often music has within it a change of quality or a shape involving different qualities in different parts, in a sandwich form, A.B.A., or in a more complex arrangement. The arts are now in partnership and both must be considered.

The music must not be too long because much movement takes place in a short time and music suffers from abbreviation or distortion.

We must consider the rhythmic quality of the music. Music may be pulsating, with strong beat, as in much 'pop' music; the beat may be strong as in marches and dance tunes; the rhythm may be more flowing or even be submerged; there may be free rhythm, the flow of the music emerging without regular rhythmic division. Music in 2/4 time or with four beats in a bar may tend to be 'square' and to hold back the flow of movement, but this is not always so. For instance, Trumpet Voluntary by Jeremiah Clarke, given the title Trumpet Voluntary by Sir Henry Wood, is an elegant marching tune which encourages control and dignity with the flow of movement held back. The Dambusters' March by Eric Coates is lively with a much quicker tempo, giving an ongoing atmosphere. Scottish reels are bouncy and encourage locomotion with a light energy. The Pavane from Warlock's Capriol Suite brings the sustainment and smooth, fine movement of the pavane as a court dance. Scott Joplin's piano rags give the liveliness of syncopation.

Music in 3, 5 or 7 time or with free rhythm usually has a flowing nature. There are waltzes such as that from Benjamin Britten's Matinées Musicales, Elgar's Bavarian Dance and simple Scottish and Irish waltz country dances. Greensleeves has a gentle, easy flow. Dave Brubeck's Take Five, some folk tunes and dances have 5, 7 or even 11 beats in a bar and give a freely flowing accompaniment. Then there is music which is free of regularity in rhythm such as Bob Downes's Open Music.

One considers the quality, the rhythmic patterns, the phrasing and the shape as a whole.

We are not attempting to dance the music, to move to each beat, to interpret its structure, but to join with the music, so that it will be a partner, giving an extra dimension, often giving security and often immense pleasure.

Where then do we look and listen? One must consider those composers who wrote music for children, Schumann, Kabalevsky, Debussy. One might listen to music played on old and interesting instruments, and to folk songs, old and new. Television theme music often brings familiarity and awakens ideas. There is a wealth of popular music with which the children may be familiar which one might use sparingly and sensitively. There is enormous scope but search can take much time and one is wise to keep ideas tucked away, like an internal library, as a teacher has stories ready for a rainy day. Sometimes the musical idea comes first and one knows that at some time that particular piece of music will be useful. Perhaps the music is the children's choice, which they have heard together or at home. Music written for dance or arising from dance-like or folk roots is likely to be 'right', Bartok's Children's Dances, music from the theme tunes of 'The Flight of the Condor' which has folk origins, folk songs from many lands and folk dances which one can use in a different way. It helps if one knows something of the work of individual composers, that a composer might offer a strongly rhythmic, dynamic sound as do Stravinsky, Bartok and Brubek quite often, or that a composer tends to give melody as can Ravel, Debussy and Delius.

Even as I write I can hear a teacher say, 'Much too difficult.' but one is sometimes amazed at the way in which children absorb the elements of music which seem complicated and even obscure. We are not asking them to analyse or to be intellectual about musical composition, but to listen, to join and to enjoy.

Then there is the exciting world of descriptive music. Composers have been inspired by the sea, fire, the machine and magic, by those things which stimulate words and story, drama and dance, painting and sculpture and which exist so vividly for children.

Such music may help the mood, deepen the experience, give landmarks to the composition, exits and entrances, beginning and end, and moments of greater and lesser energy, of climax and conclusion. Examples of such descriptive music exist in Britten's Peter Grimes, Grieg's Peer Gynt, Saint Saen's Carnival of the Animals and Milhaud's La Creation du Monde. Descriptive music abounds in both past and present composition.

Not all dramatic dance needs music. Sounds from the voice, percussive sounds from body or from instruments available, or indeed no sound at all, may be the best partnership for the whole or part of a composition.

One should emphasize the need for thought and care when choosing music for dance. What kind of sound is needed to relate to the movement? Each of us has individual feeling about music and as we work together sensitive decisions have to be made for all. Do we need the spacious soaring of melody as played on a violin, the deep richness of a cello or a bassoon, the subtle purity of a guitar, or does the dimension of the dance require an orchestra? Whatever sound stimulates or accompanies dance, in the end it must both accompany and stimulate. It must be used with sensitivity and respect for both music and dance.

For young children, perhaps especially, its use will be sparing. They have so much to experience in their movement which must be free from sound, and some which can go alongside music if the choice is well made. Children have real experience of music and come to know it and to love it when it is a partner for their dance.

Some Suggestions about Music

One hesitates to produce a list of music which teachers might introduce to children to stimulate or to accompany their dance. So much is a question of personal choice, availability, the need of the moment and the age and musical experience of the children. So, one writes with some hesitation, urging that music is used with care and sensitivity and that parts are chosen so that the quality and wholeness of the episode extracted are not spoiled.

It is again necessary to emphasize the value of the use of the voice in an expressive and rhythmic way, and that 'doodling' sounds, chanting operatic style and repeated words can offer stimulus and accompaniment. Teacher and children can use such sounds.

Songs, jingles and rounds will be sung in the classroom, at assemblies, in the cloakroom and playground. One can often use these for dance, in fact the children do so quite naturally.

Recordings can be made of children's sound compositions for use with their dance. This is important because although dancing and singing can be good partners and children move and take breath in phrases, moving with prolonged effort as in continual running or jumping makes singing very difficult or impossible.

Here are a few examples of music which is recorded. There is a wealth of such music and this is only an attempt to indicate that wealth. There will be much 'pop' music, television theme tunes and other music which is contemporarily popular. Folk dances, jigs and reels are recorded in collections, usually indicating their countries of origin.

Arnold, M.	English and Scottish Dances	Varied in tempo and texture.
Alpert, H.	Tijuana Brass A Taste of Honey, Nursery Rhymes	Lively rhythms and some familiar melodies.
Beethoven, L. van	Pastoral Symphony, no. 6	Peaceful music, some merry dances, storm.
Bernstein, L.	West Side Story Fancy Free	Excitingly dramatic. Lively rhythms.

Bizet, G.	Jeux D'Enfants	Varied ideas. Simple in structure.
Britten, B.	Four Sea Interludes from Peter Grimes	Interesting, fine, descriptive music.
	Songs from Friday Afternoons	Songs are beautifully and clearly sung. The children will know and sing some of them.
	Matinées Musicales Soirées Musicales	Some clear rhythms. Varied textures.
Carter, S.	Songs of Faith and Doubt sung by Donald Swan	Songs with a 'message'. Very clear and often simple in structure.
Collins, J.	Songs of the Folk Years	Sung sensitively. As in Turn! Turn! Turn! and Farewell, the idea is very simple.
Copland, A.	Appalachian Spring	Some descriptive music. The tune used for 'Lord of the Dance' is here in canon form.
	Two Dance Episodes from Rodeo	Lively and exciting.
Debussy, C.	La Mer Nocturnes	Mood music, interesting in shape and development.
Dukas, P.	The Sorcerer's Apprentice	Exciting, dramatic.

Elgar, E.	Three Bavarian Dances	Lively, rhythmic dances.
Falla, M. de	Ritual Fire Dance from El amor brujo	Exciting dramatically and rhythmically.
Fauré, G.	Pavane Berceuse in D major	Quiet, gentle, calm.
Grainger, P.	Duke of Marlborough Fanfare	Includes many pieces with folk origin. Rhythmically clear and simple.
Grieg, E.	Peer Gynt Suite no. 1. Elegiac Melodies	A variety of ideas. Some are simple in rhythm and structure.
Hérold, V.	La Fille mal gardée	Some folk melodies and lively dances such as the clog dance.
Holst	The Planets Suite	Descriptive, exciting, varied in texture.
Joplin, S.	Elite syncopations	Rag time gaiety, with some variation of mood.
Mozart, A.	Six Contradances March no. 1 in D. Eine Kleine Nachtmusik also Eine Kleine Beatle Music directed by Fritz Spiegl	Many dance ideas. Simple in form and rhythm.
Munrow, D.	Sixteenth Century Dances played by renaissance bands	Very attractive and interesting sound. Simple rhythm.

Mussorgsky, M.	Night on the Bare Mountain Pictures at an Exhibition	Full of 'colour'. Varied and dramatically exciting.
Poulenc, F.	Les Biches ballet suite	Very rich in texture. Lively in parts.
Purcell, H.	Music for Trumpet	The trumpet gives a special strength sometimes.
Saint-Saens, C.	Carnival of the Animals	Varied, descriptive. Children enjoy the episodes as they recognize the animals portrayed.
Schumann, R.	Scenes from Childhood Papillons	Some are short enough to be used complete. Varied in texture.
Sibelius, J.	Finlandia The Swan of Tuonela	Mood music, somewhat sombre but exciting musically.
Vaughan Williams, R.	Fantasia on Greensleeves	A well known melody beautifully arranged.
Warlock, P.	Capriol Suite	Dances, beautifully arranged give varied rhythms and textures.

CHAPTER 9

Using Words with Movement and Dance

Movement is the first language and it is where all children can begin. So it can initiate and further the language of words. A child's ability to be able increasingly to handle words, first verbally, then written, is desperately important. The plights of the poor reader in school and of the semi-literate adult are severe. We must use words in abundance and in conjunction with meaningful experience. Movement teaching is associated with description, with discussion, with the stimulus of ideas expressed in words, poetry and story. Movement itself does not need words. It is a 'language' which can go further in its meaning than can words, but the very fact that it does not need the word language means that the young child can begin to use ideas for which he does not yet have words. What a child does in his movement happens through himself, through his body, his initiative, his energy and his control. There is no intermediary material and the result is that of dynamic experience.

A teacher of young children knows how they love the sound of words, their rhythm and repetition. She knows that words must pour out from her and that she must have a patient, listening attitude to children's own struggles to put words together.

As we have seen, we must name with the child the parts of his body as they become important in movement. 'Our feet are soft and quick.' 'Now they are big and strong.' We describe our feet. What about Mrs Button's poor feet for our youngest children?

When Mrs Button of a morning
Comes creaking down the street,
You hear her old two black boots whisper
'Poor feet, poor feet, poor feet'.

When Mrs Button every Monday
Sweeps the chapel neat,
All down the long hushed aisles they whisper
'Poor feet, poor feet, poor feet'.

Mrs Button after dinner,
(It is her Sunday treat),
Sits down and takes her two black boots off
And rests her two poor feet.

But our feet can run and jump and tread softly. Our hands can
work, make shapes, stroke and grasp; knees and elbows can
make points. The names of some parts of the body are among the
earliest words a child speaks. As he comes to move with greater
skill and variety, words which describe pour in, and as movement quality becomes more refined, vocabulary grows further.
We become quick, fast, rapid, or slow, calm or smooth. One
makes the body strong, hard, tense, tough, or light, soft, delicate.
One becomes big, huge, or small, tiny, spread out or closed in,
wide or narrowed, twisted or straight, near to the floor, low
down, nearer to the ceiling, high up. Words come from teacher
and children, not just single words but many words and descriptive terms which enrich the whole idea as well as the word language for the children. Movement may be roundabout, twisting
and turning, not going anywhere, enjoying the space. Strong
position may be firm, rooted to the ground, not to be knocked
over, hard and tough. One describes movement in the language
of every day. Do not let us introduce a movement jargon.

Movement means action so we run, travel, step, prance, hop,
jump, leap, creep or crawl. We punch, hit, slash, push, stroke,
feel, spin, stretch and shrink, open and close. Words, their
meanings and their sounds, become alive for children. We can
see if understanding is there and can help immediately if there is
misunderstanding. Asian children misunderstood the word
backwards, coming back to me, until we had stepped backwards
up the hall many times. A group of children at the top of the
junior school, expressing the word tortuous, made an exciting

drama with a victim tied to a stake. It was vivid and imaginative but made obvious the need to clarify the meaning of this word. Movement can so well be tortuous.

Children's love of the sound of words sometimes overwhelms and precedes the need for meaning. I said to a group of children, 'Let's make a lovely finale'. Then quickly realizing my use of words said 'Let's make a lovely ending'. But one child at least had heard and had loved the first word. She whispered afterwards, 'Didn't we do a lovely finale?'. The rhythm of words is captured with the rhythm of movement. So a child with a short leg and a consequent marked limp enjoyed very much his walk along the corridor to a song-like chant, 'Here we come, here we come, to the hall, to the hall'. The important thing was that the accent was upon the good leg so that the short one did not dip so markedly. Therapy can be fun.

Words arise with movement in children's play, in their singing games and as they create dance and drama. Movement and sound, including words, grow alongside one another, the natural attitude to play can be called upon. Effort is required, concentration is there, the quality of what happens must be the best that can be given, but it can be fun and the barriers to learning need not be too difficult for all to surmount.

One may make a more deliberate link. Stimuli for movement and dance, for the making of sequences and of compositions of a fuller nature are many. It may be the movement idea itself, there may be a dramatic idea, shape or a design, there may be sound or music, or it may be that the stimulus is the spoken or written word, preferably both.

One can ask children to create their movement from a single word. Such a word might be written clearly and beautifully on a card which they handle, or on the board. It may be a descriptive word, smooth, jerky, alert, dreamy, exploding, expanding, rushing, searching. There may be a sentence 'We come together from far places in the room.' 'Together we make a very strong shape.' 'We are in a procession, going through the town.' 'We are like the shape of a wrecked ship lying on the ocean bed.' 'We move across the hall as fast as a lightning flash.' 'We run, leap and fall, and roll over until we are still.' Such sentences can be written or verbal and can be as simple or as complex as is desirable for group work with a particular class or for a particular child within a group.

Poetry and dance seem so often to 'speak' in the same way. Stimulus for movement and dance composition might come from poetry.

Slowly

Slowly the tide creeps up the sand,
Slowly the shadows cross the land,
Slowly the cart horse pulls his mile,
Slowly the old man mounts the stile,
Slowly the hands move round the clock,
Slowly the dew dries on the dock,
Slow is the snail, but slowest of all,
The green moss spreads on the old brick wall.[1]

One might have to discuss cart horses and indeed in our inner cities the dew and the dock.

The Sea

Lashing, clashing against the rocks,
The tumultuous sea revenged itself,
Pulling, pushing with all its mighty strength,
It circles, twists and entwines,
A sudden explosion and all is still.

A child's poem

Red Devils

Red devils dancing round a fire,
Flames flashing, limbs leaping higher,
Toes twitching, ears pricked erect,
Red devils cinder flecked

Violet Bruce

A teacher would have to decide if and when she offers this.

Cats

Sleeping, waking,
Giving such tremendous yawns
The cat goes courting!
Disturbed, the cat
Lifts its belly
On to its back.

Japan (18th century)

One finds children's own poetry is stimulating and right for children's movement creation.

Red

Red is a strong colour.
It is like fire.
It is like blood.
Red is like a barrier of anger.
Red is a jagged colour.

A child's poem

My own poem about the Snow

The snow came gently falling, with its flakes dancing and
    twirling,
Its rays shining and glistening,
Gently it falls.
You touch it and it is softly white velvet,
Cold as ice,
As beautiful as peacock feathers,
Slowly it reaches the ground,
Settles, there,
And quietly sleeps.

A child's poem

You need hands to pull things
You need hands to push things
You need hands to rip things
You need hands to grip things
You need hands to help
You need hands to clap
You need hands to balance
You need hands to catch
You need hands to feel
You need hands to touch
I like my hands very much.

David Spencer, 6 years

It may be that the work is preceded by movement study of quality or action; for instance, poems about the sea and snow might well follow work on strength and power, fineness and delicacy in movement; poems about slow things and swift things, work on time; Red Devils might occur near to Hallowe'en and might be associated with the study of movement accenting different parts of the body, from pointed shape, or from different ways of jumping.

The word stimulus might well be from a book which is being read, a description, or an event.

An extract from An Enchanted Garden

The whole of the bottom of the lagoon, as we called the calm water within the reef, was covered with coral of every shape, size and hue. Some portions were formed like huge mushrooms; other appeared like the brain of a man, having stalks or necks attached to them; but the most common kind was a species of branching coral, and some portions were lovely pale, pink colour, others were pure white. Among this there grew large quantities of sea-weed of the richest hues imaginable, and of the most graceful forms, while innumerable fishes, blue, red, yellow, green and striped, sported in and out among the flower beds of this submarine garden.[2]

Children will talk and write about their movement and dance and that which has excited them.

> To run, jump, freedom, wander, wonder,
> Walk, universe, field, float, drift,
> Silently exploring space.
> To be free.
> I ran, ran, exploring the land,
> Wondering where freedom began.
>
> *A child's poem*

Space	space	space
Move	move	move
Slow	slow	slow
Jump	jump	rest
Look	look	search
Silence	silence	freedom.

Such a wealth of words is exchanged, discussed, explored and loved as children work in the classroom, in the hall and back in the classroom again.

Dance does not need to rest upon the dramatic idea but it is in the nature of the arts and indeed of children that there is no rigidity. The arts are very close, but just as dance does not need to be dramatic in the usual sense, drama can exist without dance as it most often does when the spoken word predominates. Dance can arise from a dramatic idea, especially when the idea asks for the body to express more fully, when words may not be enough. Dance form arises from ideas of nature, the wind, storm, the sea; from the movement and flight of animals and birds; from the supernatural and from magic; from the miracles of science, from machinery, from outer space; from feelings and experiences, from the real and imagined world. A teacher will observe and will listen to children. She will know about some of the things which they have encountered, which have interested or excited them, which perhaps have puzzled them, and will be able to help them to express in dance or drama, in paint or words.

At the early stages many things may be happening in a dance class at the same time. One child may be moving softly and quietly, while another may say, 'I am a burglar'. Strength may bring about simply the strongest that a child can be, as himself, while another becomes a spider man.

When setting forth to use dramatic ideas to stimulate dance a teacher must choose carefully but not be disturbed if the response of the children is not what she envisaged. Sometimes a story is best told. It might be expressed in a collage or a picture. Some situations inspire conversation and words are sufficient. Mime enters quite often as the way in which children can express what they understand. Sometimes children cannot extend their understanding to the dance 'language'. For instance, children faced with the story of the Good Samaritan did not dance about passing by and gathering in care, but acted out the situation, miming rather than speaking because the teacher had asked them to make a dance.

Dramatic ideas have a prominent part to play in the dance activities of young children so long as we ensure that the progress of movement education matches and enriches the stimulus, that arts are allowed to blend, the distance between them being small, and that often dance is about movement itself, about energy, space and form, and about relating with others, and so often does not need a story.

We do not set out to become the sea, the dark wood or the wind, but try to find the qualities involved. The sea goes on for ever, always moving, sometimes calm, sometimes rough, so we go smoothly, on and on, to and fro, we rise and sink, jump, fall, tumble and roll as the sea hits rocks. We try to take upon ourselves the ever flowing sea. Trees are still and strong with shapes which are clear and stark in winter. Wind has its own quality, be it soft and gentle, angry or vicious. It blows through an alley, straight along. It blows everything about. The movement is embedded within the movement and ideas and understanding are enriched by the movement. It is true that with very young children it is hard to distinguish when the time of being another creature or a phenomenon of nature changes to taking upon oneself the qualities involved. Little children do become the elephant, the ghost, the twisted tree, but as we proceed they take upon themselves that which belongs, to the fog, the water or to the fire flames.

Using dramatic stimuli for movement and dance does need care for what is to be important. Often it is the essence of a story, descriptive passage or dramatic idea which we use. Using the poem 'Slowly' one does not want the children to interpret each line, but to use the idea of taking time, of smoothness and sustainment. One must emphasize the existence of the arts of drama, of mime and of dance and of their combinations. Sometimes a situation may be wholly suitable to spoken drama; the argument about the new jacket or the pocket money, Red Riding Hood's conversation with the wolf, the story of a holiday. Many stories and ideas demand words and action and are not readily suitable for dance. Mime is an art form which young children embrace very readily. Sometimes mime is almost dance as it is when Marcel Marceau performs his Pantomimes. Dance offers great licence and we can play with an idea, extend it and allow it to involve the movement capacity of the human body in its full versatility. Drama, mime and dance merge easily and one need not be too anxious about the borderlines, but must recognize where the accent lies, upon acting, upon mimetic action, upon dance. There may be a combination of these three, of words which predominate, of mime and of dance, even in one piece of work. When using the Creation Myth from the Gilbert Islands with a junior class, the worship of sun, moon and stars became dance, the lifting of the sky from the earth became mime and children also used words like 'It is stuck, I cannot lift it'. For these children the arts became a whole and any academic division would have been inappropriate.

Children talk, write, paint, act and dance about those things which interest them and about which they feel deeply. Teachers instigate and coach where the children's needs and the learning process indicates.

References

1 James Reeves, (1958). *Puffin Quartet of Poets*, Penguin Press, Harmondsworth.
2 R. M. Ballantyne, from *The Coral Island* (1860) in *A Book of Delights*, John Hadfield, Hulton Press Ltd.

CHAPTER 10

Planning and Progress

There may be, of necessity, some repetition of previous observations in this summary, but it would seem wise to remind
ourselves of the children for whom we have concern, of the rapid
development that takes place while they are in the primary school
and of their delight in the learning process.

At the nursery age we have a delightful play situation. Some
children will of course take time to acclimatize while the place and
people are strange and even rather frightening and may not join
in a movement-play session. Sooner or later the child who has
been sitting by the wall will emerge and begin to participate.
Usually it is best to wait for this to happen, remembering that a
child may join in one day and withdraw the next. Persuasion
must be subtle and gentle. One hardly needs to tell a teacher of
nursery children how to befriend the very young. I did once have
in a group a child who insisted that his father did not allow him to
dance, but he very soon joined in.

Very young children are ill-balanced, steps are taken on a large
base and they often prefer the floor, particularly if it is a shiny,
smooth one. A carpeted floor is soft and cosy but beware
brushing upon it with the bottom, body or feet as 'burns' can
occur. Movements which rise up and return to the floor are fun,
involve an exciting sense of risk, but end in security. The space
may seem very large and children tend to stay close together and
close to teacher or helper, wherever she may be. They begin to go
from end to end of the hall, to hide and to come back to teacher as
she changes her place. Many games can help them to become
confident and aware of the space. They certainly will not go out
into space and use it freely at first.

Figure 8 'High' when only five. The heels leave the floor but she is not very confident.

Figure 9 This girl leaps high and forward with the arms helping her leap.

There is little resilience; walking, running and jumping are 'flat'. Balance is insecure and the insecurity of being big, tall, wide or high must return to small, to the floor.

Stillness is a game of statues. Going and stopping, hiding parts of the body and bringing them out, shaking and being still, all are the beginning of body awareness. Extremes of quality and space are important and bring success.

They have much fun with dramatic ideas, the characters in a story, or seen on television, or in a picture. They observe, imitate and play. They love sound and respond in their own way, very varied, but quickly copying, sometimes surprising.

It is a wonderful beginning and with the same playful attitude but with thoughts of progress, teachers must try many things, listening to children's ideas, which are insistent anyway.

It is important to balance excitement with calm as far as is possible, recognizing that excitement may grow quickly and that there is no harm as teacher has perhaps to end the activity in the hall for the day. One must also be aware when concentration is waning rather than hesitate until it is gone.

Nursery children need a period in a suitable space every day, but it may well be their own familiar space which can be clear and safe enough for them to enlarge their activity.

If children have not been in the nursery, at five and six the previous characteristics will probably prevail, but new arrivals quickly progress with other more experienced members of the group.

There now develops good use of the large space and more courage to pursue a lone pathway. Body awareness, particularly of those parts which are named and are readily available, hands, feet, elbows, knees, head and faces, develops quickly. The middle of the body may be still 'hard to find'. It is often difficult for children to isolate a part of the body, but they make a part important, involve the whole of the body and its possibilities of shaking, stretching, curling, travelling and shaping. Balance becomes more secure and 'high up' is managed with more poise. Resilience is still lacking for most children and much can now be done to foster mobility and strength in the feet and legs in stepping, running and jumping. Children can manage quick travelling and tend to run over the hall, then quickly round and round in a circular pathway. Skipping from foot to foot is not usually mastered at this stage. There is the beginning of sensitive qualitative work, strong, soft, quick, still, smooth, all are attained well at extremes.

Play with words, story, character and ideas from the environment abound and the resulting exploration in movement becomes more complete in phrasing, in 'sentences' rather than 'words'. Children talk about what they do and it becomes an integrated part of their school day.

They respond to many different kinds of sounds; beating, shaking, ringing, and to music. Movement will not be linked with the outside rhythm in an 'accurate' way, but an awareness of the quality of sound is developing. They are excited by music, find it pleasurable and are urged to move from a very early stage. It is not important that the music is not 'used' in what might be thought an acceptable way.

Children still tend to copy one another but are becoming bolder in movement ideas and in space.

Again it is very important to observe the level of concentration and to balance the work with the changing mood, going with it and urging change where necessary. A daily period is necessary if possible, but young children need to change their activity when necessary so movement may take place at any time, even in one corner of the room while other things are going on around. A teacher may feel the need to allow for movement as the conversation or process of discovery demands. With the very young it is a pity if the 'movement lesson' has to wait for the allotted time in the hall.

By the time the children are seven and onwards most groups can use the large area fully, finding space and moving among one another with ease, even though they may need reminding often to find more space and to spread out. They can move with awareness of the shape of the room, its longest pathways, its centre and its edges. They become able to travel with reasonable ease forwards, backwards, sideways, turning and weaving among one another.

Body awareness is more developed and children become more conscious of the centre of the body, its front, back and sides, the shoulders and the pelvis. Stillness is well accomplished and there is increasing ability to manage more difficult balances which have smaller bases and are further from the floor.

The quality of movement is used in a more flexible way, changing from strong, to light, to heavy; accelerating and stopping, changing and using speed in a variety of ways. Phrases of movement begin to be mastered and to be repeated with increasing perfection. There is greater, more imaginative and knowledgeable use of the space around the body in gesture, children reaching out into space with clarity and increasing range.

Children progress to work with partners, in three's and a little later in groups, exploring and creating, discussing, planning and recreating.

There is increasingly meaningful and sensitive response to sounds and to simple phrasing and for most the ability to ally movement to simple sound rhythms beings to arrive. There will still be times when movement is individually, rhythmically free for all.

The lesson can usually increase in length. Concentration, though variable, persists through 'warming up', work with a special theme or idea into exploring and creating, however brief and simple. At the top of the junior school children can often work with concentration for thirty or even forty minutes.

Discussion about ideas and about the work achieved develops with children's expertise and language fluency, and time must be found for conversation even if it is postponed until all have returned to the classroom, to save time, when the space can be available for others.

There is tremendous variation in the rate of progress for young children, often greater than would appear reasonable. It depends upon the work done in the school from the earliest years and therefore upon teachers' abilities and enthusiasms. In some schools children experience movement, dance, drama and music in abundance. They see it happening around them. Professional groups may visit and teach. Video tapes and films may be watched and discussed. Visits may be made to theatre or local festival. The region and the school have their special occasions, at Christmas, Divali, Harvest and other such celebrations. In some schools drama, dance and children's music contribute regularly to assembly, and there are opportunities for the presentation of work in the arts to other classes. In some areas there is much activity beyond the normal school programme. Festivals and performances where schools join together require much extra time and opportunity to work in a communal space. Costume and properties become an important part of the performance and many people are involved. Festival and theatre are comprehensive artistic affairs with paint, material, music and perhaps drama, dance and music all playing a part. In optimum situations some primary children may reach an exciting ability to use their skills and they have a valuable experience at this early age. In past decades one might have argued that young children are not ready to present their work in this public way and that such situations are forced and perceived in an adult fashion. However, ideas and indeed the developmental time needed for children change. The environmental stimuli have changed and one can only try to balance the advantage or trauma for the few with the needs of all primary children.

There are many schools where movement and dance and indeed, drama and music play little part in the school life. This does not mean that the school is not happy, full of colour and activity. But they are artistically deprived. The school may be cramped, having too few facilities and no staff who are confident enough to begin to teach the practical arts, with the exception of the visual arts which abound in such beauty in primary schools almost without exception.

Fully anticipated and detailed planning presents a problem when one is dealing with an area of work which depends so much upon the immediate and developing needs of children, where measurement is not easy, which must be the servant and master of each individual child as far as is possible. To ensure that the teaching is positive, purposeful and progressive, however, it is essential that one works with a secure plan as a possibility and guide.

As with all teaching we are involved in a creative process. One would not wish to try to predict progress and needs with rigidity. So, we must have a programme which although clear in its fundamental pathway can be interrupted or re-structured as the needs of the week, day or moment demand or indicate. This means that the teacher must have knowledge which will allow for such change, for need, impulse and spontaneity. When one is experienced, such ease of adaptation comes readily to a teacher, particularly in the primary school, but in early days of teaching it is necessary to prepare in greater detail and to stay more firmly within the bounds of preparation for most. The natures and temperaments of teachers are as variable as those of children. Circumstances can be changeable and work in the primary school is nothing if not adaptable.

The main movement themes which underly the work at this stage are:

Awareness of the Body See Chapter 5.
The Use of the Space of the Room See Chapter 6.
Locomotion, Elevation, Ways of Travelling and Jumping See Chapters 4, 5 and 6
The Use of Varying Directions and Levels See Chapter 6.
Movement Qualities, Coordinations and Transitions See Chapter 6.
Simple Aspects of Space around the Body See Chapter 6.
Control and Freedom of Movement See Chapter 6.
Shape of the Body in Stillness, in Pathway, on the Ground and Through the Air See Chapters 6 and 7.
Partner and Group Relationship See Chapter 7.
Basic Body Actions See Chapters 4, 5, 6 and 7.

Allied with and involved will be rhythm and sound, dramatic ideas, history, geography and environmental study and activity, words, poetry, story, painting, modelling and design. Events in the world, weather conditions, sudden interests or excitements and children's ideas of all kinds mean that the exact programme may be interrupted for a valuable piece of exploration and perhaps creative work. There will be periods of steady growth and times of climax. There will be much re-teaching and 'over-learning', because we all know that it takes time for material to enter the sphere of learned experience and much teaching must inevitably 'flow away', only a little at a time being firmly retained. It is often the teacher who is bored with an idea which children wish to repeat. On the other hand a teacher must be aware when an idea has been pursued to its limit and can contribute no more for the moment. At this stage the created form or even the exploration acquires a dead quality which a sensitive teacher can well sense.

All teachers have special abilities and loves and the work can only be influenced beneficially by them. A musician or lover of music will use sound and music with care and expertise, a lover of art might venture into the making of masks and into painting and modelling in relation to the work in movement and dance. A school staff will be made up of people who have varying abilities. One can help another and children benefit as they pass from one year to another.

Now let us look at the plan of the lesson. As with all activity each lesson will have an introduction, getting ready, a transition from that which has gone before. Then there will be a period of study, working on a theme or themes. Then comes the final part when an idea comes to fruition or begins to work towards creation. One speaks of creation in the fullest sense. The lesson may be only fifteen minutes for the youngest children, but might be forty minutes long for those in the junior school. These times must be as flexible as is possible. There may be days when five minutes is enough for nursery children and days when if the space is available the work can go on until children have reached a relevant stopping place. It is a pity when concentration is acute and work unfinished to interrupt any activity and this is the joy of working in a nursery room where such flexibility of programme can be possible. We do, however, have to learn to time our work so that children have a sense of completion and acquire the discipline of using time well.

The introduction to a lesson is very important, setting the tone and attitude. Children may be excited and noisy as may be on a windy day or before a holiday. Transition needs to be made to quiet, concentrating calm, yet one must keep in mind the need of the children to let out their energy and excitement, to explode purposefully and safely. So, a quiet voice is important. Calm may come about if movement is closed in, perhaps low down, near to the floor, or if the explosive movement is controlled to phrases of going and stopping and holding stillness before going again. A wise teacher ensures calm before the children enter a large space which tends to excite anyway. Children may be in a sluggish mood needing teacher's energy to shake out the lethargy and to enliven body and mind. As we have seen, there is a two way pathway. Excitement brings excited movement, the excited movement itself creates inner excitement. A calm mood expresses itself in calm movement, and quiet, sustained movement brings about inner calm. As all teachers know a loud, excited voice only raises the noise level and disturbance if it already exists in a class. Excitement and calm are both necessary and healthy in balance and when relevant.

The introduction to the lesson then will be warming up on a cold day, then awakening and mobilizing, stretching and travelling and effecting the necessary transition from what has gone before. Very soon children will do part of this preparation for themselves as they come into the hall having changed. With younger children a teacher may well be occupied helping children with their clothes. She may feel it necessary to hold all children back so that all can enter together. She may be able to allow the children to begin their introduction so that she can finalize the process when all are ready.

In a short lesson, the introduction might take only a few moments, but it is important that it is adequately done on any particular day. It may be a more lengthy part of a longer lesson involving movements devised to correct or to challenge. It may merge into the main part of the lesson picking up the theme or themes to be studied.

Children come to understand how one begins a lesson. One must always loosen joints, muscles and ligaments, one must stretch out the body, then one can begin to run and jump. The whole body must be involved in the introduction.

The theme or themes of a lesson occupy a very important place. They will usually dominate the teaching part of the programme. There will nearly always be a main theme and other themes which are combined, associated and necessary for the balance of movement; for instance, the main theme may be the shape of the body in stillness, but lightness and strength and levels may become involved. One would not wish to concentrate wholly upon power and tension without conscious attention to relaxation and other degrees of energy. One might teach closing in the body, but it would be necessary to concentrate upon spreading out also. One must often use contrast, from closed to open, from high to low, from strong to heavy. All movement themes involve energy, time and space, whatever one's main accent may be. The main idea might be partner relationship and many themes would enter. Children might consciously and unconsciously be using varying qualities, patterns of locomotion and shape, for example.

Now we look forward to the part of the lesson which we might call the creative part, the culminating achievement for that lesson. Timing may vary. It may be that the main thematic part of the lesson leaves only a short time for creative work. This may be an unsatisfactory situation and a teacher must conclude with a sequence which sums up temporarily. Sometimes a teacher knows that the creative work or dance in hand must predominate and only a short time must be spent on the first parts of the lesson. A teacher must be free to adjust the parts of the lesson, one flowing into the other, according to the stage which the children have reached and the nature of the work in hand. We do not have rules, only guidelines.

Every lesson should, wherever possible have some work which is securely guided and some which allows for exploration, creation or children's inventiveness. Freedom to create only comes about in security, so the framework must fit the children and the situation. The climax of a lesson is often at the end as children complete their work, and perhaps show it alone, in pairs or groups. It may, however, be the middle of the lesson which is most exciting, fullest of effort and reward.

It is important that the lesson comes to a satisfying and quiet ending, making the transition to the next activity, so that the children do not rush away at the sound of a bell or as teacher has suddenly noticed the clock. It takes experience to keep a lesson within the time available and to ensure its completion, but usually children are reasonable and even a premature ending can be calm and can have the feeling of a temporary stop, to be continued. Always the end of a lesson must indicate completion. Sometimes the performance of the created work makes a satisfactory end. Sometimes one teaches a simple, easily achieved movement so that breathing becomes steady, the muscles easy and the body poised.

So we must plan carefully, observe well and note progress after a lesson so that the next lesson and the plan for the future can be purposeful.

How do I as the teacher ensure progression for the children? This is a frequent and natural question. Progress is a natural development, assisted by teaching, and the movement and artistry which comes about with such richness results from the onward processes of growing up and from the environment which we try to provide.

Bodies grow in size, legs grow longer, the centre of gravity is further and further from the ground. Coordination develops naturally and more keenly with our help. Muscles grow in strength as the body becomes increasingly secure and skilful. Progress is in the body itself, in its capabilities and powers. Children in the primary school, especially by the time they are juniors, show remarkable variation in growth pattern, in physical development, coordination and skill. Changes may appear to be sudden and leaps in achievement of skill are made. These changes sometimes are due to confidence and may be the result of success, so a teacher must use observation and skill especially where less able children are concerned.

Progress is in the quality of what is done. It is particularly in transition, in passing from one action to another, from stillness to movement to stillness, from stretching high to sinking down, to rolling over to rising again. It is in the quality of stillness. It appears in the use of 'pastel shades' of movement rather than in the extremes. One sees moderate strength, swinging heaviness, bouncing lightness, acceleration and deceleration, crescendo and dying away. Phrasing becomes more complex and climax more clear. Progress is in the involvement of the whole body, in sensitivity, in concentration, in preparation and recovery.

Progress is in relationship. A very small child moves within the crowd but does not yet really relate to the others. Children grow through their movement play with a partner to work in three's and in groups. They do not only become aware and learn to cooperate, but develop a sensitive, reacting relationship, giving and taking, leading and responding, exploring, planning and creating together, contributing special talents and having regard for those in others. So, by junior school children come to create in groups and teacher may stand further back, waiting and observing when sometimes the children take over, until there is need for her to step in to guide the progress further in terms of movement, language, clarity or creation.

There is progress in the rhythmic nature of movement. The flow and nuance becomes more fluent, children are able to control and to shape impulse and the holding back of their movement. The body becomes more able to deal with its weight as it balances and moves in ever more exciting ways.

Movement memory reaches for many a very good level and

one can be surprised at the ability children have to retain phrases, whole dances and dance dramas with accuracy.

Musicality develops and from the small child for whom rhythmic sound was exciting, for whom it meant starting and stopping, there comes about the knitting of movement and sound more closely in stimulation and accompaniment. The movement behaves more intimately, accent and phrasing are more consciously registered. Children can use percussion instruments creatively and sensitively, to dance and play with skill, perhaps bringing in recorders and portable instruments which they are learning to play. They will use their voices as the most intimate instruments they possess. So the children may be accompanying movement with sound, making sounds which stimulate movement, taping their compositions and making dances where instruments are intimately involved.

They are able to use a larger framework from which they can create. When they had little movement language it was necessary for the framework to be smaller, allowing enough freedom for children's ideas, but with the provision of security and safe feeling. Later the outline plan within which they create can be much more open. They can cope with more freedom.

Progress cannot be to order, written out list-wise. There are periods of hesitation, spurts of energy and achievement and times when all seems to be standing still. There must be times of consolidation. There may well be the need to go back, to re-do, to repeat or to leave. We 'over-learn' and something of what we achieve will stay. As we go along, the language learned, the relationships achieved, the skill acquired, spatial knowledge experienced, all are to be used in creating, with more complex material, shaping, sounds, words and ideas, with more and more confidence and ability to communicate.

The body changes and acquires coordination and skill, the craft of dance develops, there are changing emotional and expressive needs and working together becomes a part of the artistic process. The world opens up for children as they live in the atmosphere of the primary school. They burst with energy, inquisitiveness and ideas which they need to express, relevantly and with clarity.

CHAPTER 11

Observation and Recording

What does observation mean for the teacher of young children? It is a term used so casually, especially to young student teachers who can hardly be expected to master all the tasks which confront a teacher in charge of many children. It is difficult sometimes to deal with all the problems and necessities as they arise and it takes time, peace of mind, a keen eye and a clear knowledge of what one seeks to observe for observation to become an accomplished art. Nevertheless observation is vital so that teaching, preparing, planning and progress may take place to the benefit of all children.

In a movement lesson children are not still for long and one's eyes must be keen, one's organized searching acute. Often teachers have said how amazed they have been by the difficulties and abilities shown by children which they have noticed on the rare occasion when able to relinquish responsibility, to sit back and really observe their children. So, when we say that teachers must observe it is with understanding of the problem.

We must stand back from time to time in a lesson. It is easy for a teacher to move too much or to give too much instruction because she is unsure and anxious. We should give children themselves a chance to observe others where relevant, remembering that young children are most anxious to do and are impatient if watching takes too long.

One becomes aware of the particular activity level of children on particular days, or times of day, and of the effects of particular aspects of school life. Sometimes it is necessary to observe an individual child even at the expense of others if one is concerned for any reason.

The human body in action attracts immediate attention. How do the children move? Are there problems with any part of the human body? One observes the symmetry of the body in its movement, particularly as a child walks and runs. Are there parts of the body which do not fully participate when one would expect them to do so? One must watch with great care and persistence because it is very easy to think that there is movement or lack of movement where the lapse has been only momentary.

One observes children's breathing. Quite often young children will become healthily breathless and breathing quickly returns to normal, so that one would be aware if any child had lasting distress in breathing after energetic movement. Teachers must be told if any child has a physical problem which might prohibit exertion. Such children usually very well protect themselves, but a teacher must observe any undue, prolonged breathlessness and any change of colour in a child's face which does not quickly return to normal.

One observes tension. What measure of extreme tension can children achieve? Can the body be strong in all its parts? Does a child carry too much persistent tension even when the task does not require it? One observes the ability to relax as it is encouraged and taught. Is any child over relaxed in movement and stance?

One is concerned with energy. Young children are naturally energetic, though fatigue can enter later in a day. A teacher will be concerned if for any child there is repeated lack of energy which may have physical origin or may be connected with mood, lack of understanding or unhappiness. We have all had children in our classes who seem to be over excited, very active, sometimes disruptive. Children are individuals with differing activity levels and temperaments. There has to be an outlet for pent-up energy, especially when children have been confined to a small classroom. In inner cities children are extremely limited for space at home and often at school, and activity is vital. It has to be controlled so that there is safety, so that movement education is pursued, so that one can allow children to go fast and to use energy, to jump and to make strong, sudden action, to be excited and energetic to the point of panting, as soon as they can use the space well enough and there can be a sure and disciplined stopping point. It is sometimes worthwhile even to keep part of the class still, close to the wall, if it gives space for a few at a time to move with greater freedom. Rarely one has a child who might be diagnosed by professionals as hyper-active. Such a child needs special help as does any child who has obvious, persistent movement problems of a marked nature.

There may of course be an excessively lethargic child. We have seen the child who seems to have little energy and whose attitude to time is slow. Such a child needs careful observation in all situations because here there is little disruption and a teacher might well not notice the sluggishness. This child might be in need of help.

Coordination in movement, the ability to use parts of the body in harmony with one another, to maintain balance of the body as it moves and the weight is transferred from part to part, from foot to foot, varies markedly and we must give time. Sometimes a child stands out because of lack of coordination and we speak of the 'clumsy' child. The condition of clumsiness, like that of hyper-activity, can be at a level which merits medical diagnosis and care, but in the mainstream of children some are clumsier than others, just as some are quicker and more active than others. Movement education seeks to help the development of coordination and balance which opposes clumsiness. We are concerned here with balance, with the intended direction of an action, with the application of appropriate degrees of tension, with the use of the right and left sides of the body in accordance with development, in the larger actions of the body. Other aspects of coordination and clumsiness become obvious in the classroom where the child is handling and placing materials. A teacher is in the fortunate position of being able to observe any child for whom she has concern, in movement and physical education lessons, and as the child uses water, sand, counters, paint brush. A teacher will observe the nature and timing of an individual child's clumsy movement when such movement is readily achieved by others. Such a child may need help.

We observe the concentration of which children are capable. This again will be immensely variable, but there may be children whose concentration wavers consistently, differing from most of the children in the class at the time. We observe too, children who are greatly absorbed. Perhaps for some children movement and dance brings the greatest absorption.

These aspects are all related and contribute to the measure of success or failure for a child. A sensitive teacher, knowing the value of success and the harm which persistent failure brings, endeavours to give all children the chance to succeed, praising when she can, giving opportunity to the less able while securing the progress of others.

One observes the relationship of children, how they cooperate with one another, those who lead and those who only follow. This tells us something of the personality of a child, possibly of his home experiences, and enables a teacher to plan and to organize her class as she tries to keep an encouraging balance.

One is bound to observe aggression and perhaps withdrawal. These particular aspects will possibly disappear quite easily as children become part of the group behaviour. Nevertheless it would be unreal to suggest that there may not in a group be a child who needs help and the more accurately a teacher has observed the more easily this help might be given.

We have spoken of the extreme difficulties which some children have. These are very important and a head teacher will be able to pass on a problem to some extent to the appropriate specialists. We are mainly concerned, however, with all the children, with normality in its immense variation, so that we may remedy our mistakes, plan our teaching, maintain progress for all and consolidate learning. We must talk with children about their experiences in the movement lesson, in the classroom, at home, during the holidays, as we continue observation wherever we can.

We observe children's interests in words, poems, stories and events that go on around them. We note words and concepts which have excited interest and those who need help which could be given through movement. Creative work is to be balanced, in mood, in size, in timbre and range. One observes the needs of children at any particular time, to work quietly and calmly, to absorb excitement, to relieve sadness and to enter into festivity.

Recording

A teacher is a busy person and will not welcome extra note making and written tasks. Nevertheless we must be sure that observation is well used and progress evaluated. Records may be required by the Head and in any case will be essential for the next teacher.

Some teachers will have greater need for detail than others. Modes of keeping records vary, but one offers the outline of a possible plan.

Suggestions are written progressively.

Bodily Movement
Hold a position
Use both sides of the body with ease
Some resilience in feet and knees
Balance briefly on one leg
Use of all parts of the body most prominent in movement
Name parts used
Skip from foot to foot
Step backwards with ease
Jump with resilience
Coordinate parts of the body in more complex movements
Turn easily and control the movement
Jump with a turn and land well
Run freely in curving and straight pathways
Use the body in symmetry and asymmetry
Control body shape in stillness

Movement Quality
Strength in stillness
Step softly
Run about the hall quickly and be able to stop
Control simple movements like stretching, creeping in a sustained manner
Move the upper limbs with softness and delicacy
Move with strength as in striking, beating, pressing and dragging
Step with strength
Run and jump with resilience and lightness
Acquire poise throughout the body
Run and jump with freedom
Control stopping from speedy and free movement

Use movement qualities in variety and transition throughout the body.

Spatial Awareness
Use the floor space well, to find a space alone
Use the space around the body in simple directions, high, low, wide, narrow
Shape the body in stillness
Use the space of the room in advancing, retreating, turning and changing direction with ease
Use the space around the body fluently in gesture
Master the transition in movement from place to place in gesture and locomotion.

Relationships
Share the space well and join in the activity throughout the lesson
Relate to teacher's guidance
Work with a partner, leading and following in locomotion, body shape and gesture
Invent sequences with a partner
Use questions and answers with a partner
Work in 3's using combinations possible with 3 people
Work in a whole group with awareness of others, using touch
Work in a smaller group, combining to create and to clarify ideas.

The Use of Sound
Stop on a signal
Respond to the quality of sound on a tambour
Respond to shaking sounds
Move in phrases as in 'move . . . and stop'
Respond to longer sounds such as those of a gong or cymbal
Use the voice accompanying movement
Use body percussion such as clapping, clicking of the fingers, sounds of feet on the floor and hands on the body
Follow a musical rhythm in stepping
Respond to musical rhythm with the whole body
Use musical form of a simple nature such as A.B.A. and use repetition in music
Use descriptive and dramatic music well.

Composition and Creative work attempted or completed for example
Sequences of strong movement
Strong statues
Choosing between strong and soft
The autumn wind
Following a partner
Question and answer with a partner
Group shapes with given titles
Group composition with percussion instruments
Dance about ghosts
Dance about the sea using own vocal sound and percussion
Dance for Christmas taking the journey of the Three Kings as
    central theme

Notes about individual children for example
J. can now skip.
M. does not join in all the time
A. has a severe problem with resilience
J. still disturbs the class and does not concentrate
G. laughs now
P. has great difficulty in controlling his body in stillness
A. finds relating to others difficult. She does not find a partner
    easily
J. reacts sensitively and eagerly to music
A. enjoys dramatic ideas and becomes cooperative.

Planning For the Term

This may be required for the school records. There should be
consultation between staff about plans to avoid undue repetition
and to ensure a rich movement education. It is not always a
happy situation to have a school plan so that a teacher has certain
parts of the work to cover, as can be possible and necessary in
some areas of learning. It is perhaps best if a teacher has great
freedom but is aware of the level of children's accomplishment
and of what she hopes to achieve with them. We must remember
that all aspects of movement ability have within themselves
much variation and scope for progression. A child might accomplish a turn with a jump but will manage it later in many
ways, with increased elevation and control in different rhythms,

in continuity with other movements and in the context of a composition. The ability to follow a partner is one thing, but to move in response, to oppose, to make and break contact, to compose a dance together is another.

One might plan under the headings suggested for recording. A teacher will know some of the highlights of the term: Divali; Christmas; a poem which one intends to read; Glaciers; Solid shapes; Symmetry.

CHAPTER 12

Planning the Lesson

One hesitates to write lesson plans. All teachers plan their lessons differently. Some plan in detail, others carry the themes in their mind and trust their ability to develop them with due regard to what occurs. The most experienced teachers, with rich knowledge, may be able to do this on many occasions with great success, the lesson flowing naturally to the benefit of all. Most teachers, however, need a firmer base and must always have a plan for a regular lesson even though much may happen spontaneously. As experience and knowledge grow lessons may depart from the plan more and more, as the development of an idea and the creativeness of teacher and children indicate.

Children love to repeat and it is necessary anyway that there should be a revision of work done and particularly a reminder of the last lesson. Sometimes one is disheartened because the quality of the achievement or even the achievement itself seems to have disappeared or deteriorated. There are many reasons why this should happen; weather, time of day, mood of the class or even of an individual, disturbance, or indeed there may be no apparent reason.

These are only suggestions about lessons as they may occur in part or as a whole. They are random samples, making no rules and creating no boundaries.

They are lessons which have taken place and which have brought about some success, some learning and much pleasure. Things happened which were not in a plan and which extended learning for teacher and children.

I have decided to write informally, almost as one speaks. This seems the best way to convey the attitude which is part of a lesson with small children. It must not be a talking down to children, only the presentation of ideas as interesting, exciting and part of learning together.

The Nursery

Much movement play happens spontaneously when a teacher feels that there is need or when it seems to be immediately relevant. Such occasions may take very few minutes and concentrated periods will probably last for ten minutes only. It is very good if for such periods children can have bare feet and a minimum of clothing, provided that conditions allow and that the teacher has sufficient help.

Space   Be prepared to repeat activities and to return to them.

Come together, very close. Go all over the room with teacher.
Teacher will shut her eyes. Go and hide. Where is teacher when you look out? Look now. Go to her.
Teacher will change her place in the room so that children go on different pathways to reach her.
Go along the smooth floor, sliding on your front or back.
Come near. Grow very big. Grow very small. Very still.

———————————

Strong, soft, quick   As above. Be prepared as children rush back to you.

Come down to the floor. Go sliding along the floor.
Come together, close. We all go together, running, with teacher, all over the hall.
You go all over the hall so softly that teacher will not hear you. She has her eyes shut.
Teacher can see you now. Come back to her very quickly.
Make very strong hands, shake them. Make strong faces. Make strong feet. Make yourself strong all over.
Fall down, slowly, into the floor. (Teacher has been reading 'All Falling Down' by Gene Zion).

———————————

Sounds Play the drum in several ways for them to listen. Introduce them to the bells, listening to the sound and the way in which it lasts.

Come together and listen to the drum.
Go all over the hall, stop still when the drum sounds, like a statue. Play the statue game, making your statue strong as the drum rumbles.
Move while the drum plays. Go everywhere.
(Children hear the drum making a beating sound, a rumbling sound and a rhythmic pattern).
Come and listen to the Indian bells. You move if you want to or just listen.

Parts of body Combine with talking about parts of the body, with words, poems and stories.

Come together.
Shake your hands, spread them, make them into fists.
Shake them again.
Lie down and shake your feet in the air. Show your feet.
Go all over the room with very soft feet.
Curl up. Play bringing out parts of the body; the hands, the face, the elbows, all of you, very big.
Come for a walk round the hall, all round the edge, then right across to the door.

Cats (Children's idea) Combine with words and stories, perhaps drawing and talking about cats at home.

Tread all over, as softly as your cat. Your hands and feet are treading.
Curl up. Stretch out, yawning after a long sleep.
Spring like the cat does, very soft.
Everthing is very quiet and soft.
The cat scuttles away from a large dog and hides.

Young Infants

Approximately fifteen minutes.

Space to ceiling to floor   Try to make the transitions from one
   activity to another easily flowing.

Warm up your bodies; hands, feet, the middle of us, all of us.
   Wriggle. Shake.
Curl up, very small; change to get bigger and bigger. Repeat
   several times, with tambour getting louder and softer.
Run all over the hall, filling it up.
Stop very still. Get ready to go again.
Don't crash into anyone. Go again.
Go down to the floor, very still, cuddle the floor. Getting taller
   and taller, reaching for the ceiling, as high as you can. Can you
   balance? Go back to the floor.
Dance to music. (Music with continuous beat.)
Come back together.

───────────────

Quick smooth

'Oil up' our bodies. Hands, feet, knees, elbow, middle.
Go all over the room. Keep it full up.
Come into the middle of the room. Now go all over it again.
Go very softly. Go very smoothly.
Talk about 'smoothly'.
Go as quickly as you can. Don't touch anyone.
Stop on drum sound.
Shake your body very quickly. Be still on the drum sound. Do it
   again.
Stand very still. Fall down very slowly on to the floor.

───────────────

Shape of body   Do not keep children in stillness too long.

'Oil up' the body. Concentrate on parts of the body; hands, feet,
   elbows, knees, shoulders, head and middle.
Go all over the room, go how you wish.
Grow very tall. Can you balance?
Change and be very small and curled up.
Going and stopping, very still, like a statue.

Try different kinds of statues; round, like an apple, or a pumpkin; very long like a lamp-post, very twisted up like the old tree up the lane.

Choose your own statue. Make it very strong and hard. Let it fall down in a heap on the floor.

Come together to talk about statues.

Winter as it came one day   This is a lesson of contrasts. Make the transitions sensitively.

'Oil up' the body, stretching and curling.

Listen to the music. Be as bouncy as you can as you go all over the room. (Pop music or jig).

Making the body very hard and sharp. Finding parts which stick out. Finding very strong, sharp movements.

Make the body very soft and round. Move softly as if through the snow on the playground before it is swept.

Talk about the winter. Make a group shape of the garden in winter, frozen until the snow came to cover it up.

Now it has changed to be soft and round. Everything is covered with snow.

Older Infants

Approximately 20 minutes.

Quick, slow, smooth   There are many changes. Try to make the lesson flow smoothly.

'Oil up' the body, part by part. Children suggest which part next. Shake the whole body free.

Listen to music. Dance all over the room. (Continuous, skipping rhythm.)

Go very smoothly. Listen to a long sound, from a cymbal or gong.

Go very quickly. Listen to your feet.

Grow very big, very smoothly. Grow very small, very smoothly. Change your shape, very smoothly.

Try all these changes, very suddenly.

Come to the back of the hall. Go up the hall together, very smoothly. Go all over the hall very quickly.

Start slowly, smoothly, now a little quicker, quicker still, **very quick**, to stop.
Come together to talk about smoothly, slowly and quickly.

Working with a partner   Make a 3 if you have an odd number, but remember the 3 as you give instructions.

'Oil up' the body, ending with going all over the hall.
Find a partner and go with your partner for a walk all over the room.
Let's number 1 and 2. Both of you will have a turn. Number 1, you lead your partner and show the way. Number 2 you lead and show your partner how you will go.
Explore making twin shapes, (teacher guiding the organization).
Explore making shapes which fit with one another. Making shapes with your partner which touch.
Finish the lesson by dancing to music by yourself.
Relax in your own space on the floor.

The dark, dark wood   Touch must be light, not leaning or tugging. You may be able to draw the curtains to make the hall dim. Do not prolong the drama and be sure that the final movement is relaxed and happy.

'Oil up' the body very thoroughly because much conversation may take place.
Making shapes which are very hard, which twist and have parts sticking out.
Making shapes which are soft and rounded.
Change from one to the other.
Close your eyes so that you can just see through your eye lashes. Move about very carefully. It is like moving in the dark.
Come together and remind ourselves about the story we have been reading.
Let us make the wood. Find your place. Make your shape.
It is a magic wood and now it begins to come alive, to move, until the cymbal sound stops it again.
Shake it all off. Come together and stand tall.

Junior children

The warm up and preparation of the body may be begun by the children themselves as they enter the hall from the changing area. Then it may become more formal, designed to improve the movement memory as one asks for sequences of movement such as, stretching, shrinking, stretching and turning, to stillness; shaking with increasing intensity, to running, leaping and falling, to stillness. Movement becomes more accurate and may be prescribed as a result of a teacher's observation of limitation, of difficulty in coordination or awkwardness of transition. One begins to deal with the safety of skills which the children themselves introduce or which are at this time consistent with the development of artistry. Landing from jumps, especially from twisting jumps, must be resilient. One may deal with skills where the weight is taken upon various parts of the body, perhaps taking them in slow motion so that problems can be discerned and eliminated. One may have to teach lifting and carrying bodies and the care which is essential for oneself and others.

Junior children come to work well in groups, to show their work and to talk about their observations of their own and others' creative ideas.

It is important to be increasingly aware of all children, to give scope for all, for the strong and energetic, and for the gentle child who works quietly and with great sensitivity. I think of the Asian girls who love the quiet sound and whose movements are shaped with care. Individual and group work make it possible to give scope to all children with their individual bodies and temperaments as one tries also to bring about a greater balance for all.

Strength in quickness and slowness. Working in groups Guide the children with your directions and rhythms.
Make cards as attractive as possible.
Decide if the groups should present their work to others.
This work may take more than one lesson.

Curling and stretching the body in standing, moving as guided through ankles, knees, hips, spine, head, elbows, wrists, fingers, to full stretch. Curling back, starting with the fingers.

Go freely all over the hall. Stop to repeat curling and stretching, in your own time.

Make strong, still shapes, relaxing and repeating as accurately as you can.
Strong action in pushing and pressing. 'Get ready and press, and release.'
Strong action in thrusting, punching and leaping. 'Prepare and thrust.' 'Get ready and jump.' Work on the transition between action.

Tasks in groups, written on work cards.
1. We jump in preparation and then leap across the hall.
2. We are lifting a great weight, together, evenly. We hold it with great strength.
3. We come together to make a strong group shape.
4. We dance to the tambour. We make strong rhythm.
   There may be time to change tasks.
   It may be necessary to have more tasks in this lesson.

Run as lightly as you can all over the hall.
Come to stillness, breath easily, stretch and stand well.

Masks   Preparing the masks for movement is very important so that frustration is avoided.

Masks are made and we have made sure that they have eye holes which are large enough and are in the right place.
We have made sure that the fastening is secure and that the mask does not slip when we move.
Put on your mask and go to look at yourself carefully in the mirror. How will you move?
Put masks away safely and try out your dance. Make a beginning and an end to your dance.
Put on your mask when you are ready to practise.
A teacher may wish that the children learn to present themselves and will need to move with the mask facing the audience.
Dance in three groups, others watching as one group dances.

Twisting and turning   There must be resilience and mobility in the body. Warm up very well.

Warm up all parts of the body and the body as a whole, making sure that the body is especially warm and supple.
Turning the body from side to side freely with a swing.
Stretching out and twisting the body so that parts face different ways. Repeat in a mobile fashion.
Spinning on the spot, coming to a stop and repeating in the opposite direction.
Turning with jump. Try different ways. Teacher may have to give technical help. Rhythmic sound may give guidance and security. 'Prepare, jump and come down.'
Come together to discuss our 'turning dance'.
Make it together, starting slowly, working up to the final jumping turns, to stillness.
There could be the use of sounds, scrapers, tambourines, drums. Children could work in groups.
Finish standing very straight.

Earth and air   Children can understand the preparatory movements. Take them into your confidence.

We have been discussing things that belong to the earth and those of the air. We have read and written some poems.
Titles are, My Kite Clouds, The Wind, Seagulls, Rocks, Trees, Green and Brown, Caves, Building.

Warm up through stretching and shrinking.
Children explore jumping and falling.
Heaviness, using body weight with relaxed attitude, using low level, using the floor to travel.
Lightness, weightlessness, moving without sound, jumping and falling, with lightness and fluency.
Work in groups with some of the poems, Caves, Building, Growing Things; Clouds, Wind.
Show your dance to the class.
To end, 'from high to low', 'from air to earth'.

Responding to percussive sounds   The transitions between sounds must be made with care. Try not to disturb the transition as instruments are changed.

'Oil up' with an accent upon stretching the limbs and the whole body, on jumping and landing.

Responding to the drum or tambour.

Teacher will play, with strong accents, with delicate fingers making soft sounds in phrases, using a variety of sounds in longer phrases.

Responding to the cymbal. Hold back long movement, keep it going, let it die away.

Responding to the rattling, disturbing sound of the tambourine. Hurry. The body is agitated.

The sounds will be played in the same order, first the tambour, then the cymbal, then the tambourine.

Move with the sounds. The tambourine will bring your movements to a stop. Listen carefully.

———————————

Making group shapes   This lesson could be linked with work in visual art where the children are observing shapes and relationships in painting and sculpture.

Warm up into vigorous activity to balance the lesson which is bound to be fairly sustained.

Running, working up to vigorous and maximum elevation.

Individually, make body shape in curving, linear and twisted shape. Take care with the process of arriving and leaving the shape, 'I go and I arrive'.

Making group shape or shapes, children joining as teacher suggests by name, by clothing colour, by birthday month. The groups may be curving or angular or twisted or as the children make them.

Look at each group to see how the spaces between bodies make shapes.

Task. Each group makes its shape using a given idea.

Outside the sports hall, a statue.

The Navigators on the cliff, a statue.

The under sea shipwreck.

The coral reef.

Show one another, taking care with the arrival of the group together and its dispersal.

Partner relationship Observe children's choices of partners. You might sensitively adjust them if a child needs special help.

'Oil up' the body with an accent upon stretching, upwards and outwards. Using the legs in taking long steps forward, backward and sideways.
Partner relationship in leading and following movement in turn. Leading and following while the follower has eyes shut. Leader take great care, use space well, taking your partner by the hand, bringing him to a safe stop. Change over. (Sometimes a soft, long sound like that of a cymbal can help to ensure concentration. A noisy atmosphere is no use.)
Making partner shapes. Opposites. Shapes touching. Shapes with great strength. Shapes with fine touch.
Responding to the drum and to the gong. Making a partner dance as question and answer between the drum dancer and the gong dancer.
Partners exploring freely, leading and following, using the hall space freely, ending as teacher quietly indicates, 'Bring it to an end now'.

A dramatic dance Watch carefully. Children become very absorbed and try out exciting movements. They must use the space well, be aware of care needed when great energy is used. A few incidents may need special help. Try not to 'ban' an activity, but find a way in which it can be done well and safely.

'Oil up' quietly and intelligently, concentrating upon parts of the body and stretching tight parts such as the backs of the legs, slowly, with firm gentleness.
Move all over the hall freely to music which has strong rhythm and gaiety.
We had talked about disasters, bombs, earthquakes, fires, storms. We discussed what kinds of movement we should need to make a dance drama called 'Disaster'. Body attitude: sharp, alert, eyes wide, listening, looking. Hiding the body for safety. Groping through tunnels and holes. Escaping to safety.

Pushing obstacles away. Dragging out injured people and
carrying them to safety, Things falling. Running fast. Leading
people out.

We tried most of these ideas out with teacher's help with
movement quality. Then we put the ideas into our picture of
disaster, children deciding alone or in groups what they would
do, when they would come in and when they would end their
movement.

Transition to dancing freely to the music we used at the
beginning of the lesson. This was unhurried, the transition
taking time for the children to adjust.

Using the music 'Drums for God' From Congo, a folk tune.
Nuyimkidila, O Clap Your Hands All Ye Peoples. Children can
quickly sense this rhythm and can try out movements almost
straightaway.

We decided to make a dance to this music. It has a very strong
accent, the rhythm being repeated throughout, backed by
singing. The music builds to a climax.

We decided that it was to be a ceremony, of people coming
together in the middle of a village. We discussed the kinds of
movement we should need. It was to be strong, 'earthy' with
jumps and steps.

Warm up had an accent upon mobility, freely flowing running
and jumping and movements on low level with strong legs.

We divided into groups and planned the way which each entry
would be made.

Each group entered in turn, danced around the hall and into the
centre where they rested on low level. When all were in, the
whole class picked up the rhythm on the spot in their
individual way.

The climax was a great rising up and sinking into the floor, in
unison.

(Teacher had always to warn when the climax was near in the
music so that the dancers could prepare low down, ready to
rise.)

Using work cards   As before, present the card with clear, good lettering. A child will read one card as the group is about to present the dance.

This was a kind of 'summing up' of work done. Cards were well presented for six groups. They were as follows.
1. We start with pointed, angular movements, we stop, then we change to softer, curving movements, come together and rest.
2. We move together. We are expressing our determination, our unity. We make a protesting dance.
3. Make a dance about the West wind which disturbs everything before it dies away.
4. We are people going along the road to town. What kind of person are you? How do you go?
5. Here is a tiny Japanese poem, 'I could eat it! This snow that falls. So softly, so softly'. Use the idea in any way you like.
6. Think about machines, their precision, their sounds, of pistons, cogs and wheels. Can you together capture the quality of the machine as it goes and stops?

The children warmed up together, then gathered in their groups to work. Teacher was there for help if they needed it and went around with interest but not interference. Percussion instruments were available.

———————

Our moon dance   This might become a production. Teacher may wish to create the ending for the children so that the part becomes unison movement and is teacher's special contribution.

We talked about man's knowledge of the moon before man landed upon it. The names given to the oceans and seas as they were observed were so lovely. We chose some of these: The ocean of storms, The sea of clouds, The sea of rains, The sea of tranquility and The sea of crises. We would use these for our group dances.
We needed to think about the qualities which would be needed; energy, gentleness, directness or roundaboutness, calm or turmoil.
We decided to make a class dance to bring everyone together at

the end. This was to be about the waxing and waning of the moon.

'O lady Moon, your horns point to the East; be increased. O Lady Moon, your horns point to the West, be at rest.'

Many junior lessons needed more than one period. Children often continued to work on their ideas in free moments. This happened particularly with the masks.

Teachers will find that their children need more or less guidance than is indicated and that their approach may be very different, in words used, in tempo and in the use of repetition.

Teachers will know their children, their needs and personalities and will be able to adjust, to make changes and develop ideas in relationship with what they do in the classroom and in the environment.

Final Thoughts

Most schools now have a large space for children to move freely. It is not always available for those who need it at a particular time but teachers in primary schools are inventive and adaptable and spaces can often be found. A space may be too large as is a sports hall, and one endeavours to 'enclose' the children so that they can communicate and be secure. An outdoor space is nearly always too vast unless one can find a corner of a field or garden with some enclosure. It is sometimes possible to transfer a dance or dance drama to an outdoor situation if that experience is seen to be valuable, but it may be wise to create the form indoors. The classroom may be too cramped, but temporarily may give necessary security and sometimes offers an opportunity for some movement when it would seem to be wise. It is worth mentioning that the space used in the everyday class does have an effect upon movement and consistent use of too cramped an area influences the use of air and floor space, the dynamic quality and particularly the freedom of flow of movement. So it is important to try to alleviate this if possible by borrowing space or visiting at intervals.

Difficulties with floors which need sweeping, rooms with too much clutter, rooms which are cold or ill-ventilated and rooms which have bad acoustics do still exist. Nevertheless there are better spaces now than ever before, allowing for more space, freedom and attention.

Children are also better equipped for movement. They often have special clothing into which they can change, giving freedom and comfort and making them feel like movers and dancers. Feet should be bare if the floor is clean so that full mobility and strength can develop and ensure greater safety if the floor is at all slippery. Children or teacher must never move in socks or tights. This is extremely slippery on most floors. Hard composition floors may well be unsuitable and if inevitable one must remember that young feet are still developing and that harsh stamping, beating or landings are traumatic if the floor has no 'give'.

Sometimes using hall lights in a certain way, drawing curtains, moving furniture to change the nature of the space, to suit a particular idea, may be good and can often be done quickly, with ease and spontaneity. For instance, the hall may be made a little more dim for the episode of 'The dark, dark, wood'. A group of children who had difficulty in relating to one another when making their group shape, succeeded when they placed it between two pillars in the hall instead of in the open space.

Sometimes costumes and 'props' can be useful even in the on-going class situation, enhancing or stimulating what the children do. Useful materials are nearly always available in the primary school. It may simply be a piece of material, a cloak, a whole parachute or a floating scarf. Many things are possible, teachers and children are full of ideas and rules need be few.

At this time we see dance becoming more comprehensive. Children are surrounded by a variety of activity and styles. They see aerobics, jazz dance, break dance, contemporary dance of all kinds as well as classical ballet, dance on skates and in gymnastics. Children incorporate into their desired movement vocabulary a variety of tricks like 'splits' and back bends. It would be unwise to pretend that these influences were not there and much better to use an enthusiasm than to forbid it. So we must enlarge the vocabulary with more quality and relevance to what the children are doing, which gives opportunity to all children, to energy and skill and which respects the child as an artist who does not need to ape adult artistry.

We have a new respect for valuable aspects of our culture, for singing games and folk dance, for dances and festivals of groups which have more lately joined us in numbers. All these are important and must find a place, but they do not replace that movement education which is comprehensive, part of physical, intellectual, artistic and aesthetic behaviour and which invades and embraces the whole of education.

We are concerned with children's learning, physical development, with their sensory growth, word language, conceptual development and with all aspects of their lives in school and in the community, with others. Movement is a very important area of experience. It is in danger of neglect in education because its value may not be obvious, especially to those who plan the curriculum. It is not easy to teach. One must be willing and able to take risks, to tolerate some untidiness and uncertainty. It is not easy to measure or even for some to perceive the need for it to be taught. One must be able to 'play' and to enjoy as children's eyes shine and as they become deeply involved with what is so intimate a part of them.

We live in a greedy, materialistic world and the arts of man are in danger of being pushed aside, being of little obvious material value. In truth they constitute the most valuable area of man's existence and contribute to the wisdom which must accompany knowledge, to the passion which must relate to and temper reason. Someone once said, 'Intellect marches, imagination rambles'. So we must help the imagination to ramble and intellect to march before and after.

> A man shall be as an hiding place
> from the wind, a covert from the tempest,
> as rivers of water in a dry place, as the
> shadow of a great rock in a weary land.
> *Isaiah, Chapter 32, verse 2.*

Useful references

Bruce, V. R. (1970) *Movement in Silence and Sound*, G. Bell and Sons Ltd, London.

Clegg, A. B. (1963) *The Excitement of Writing*, Chatto and Windus, London.

Jordan, D. (1966) *Childhood and Movement*, Blackwell and Mott, London.

Harrison, K. (1986) *'Look, Look, What Can I Do?'*, BBC.

Morris, H. (1964) *Where's that Poem. An Index of Poems for Children.* Basil Blackwell, London.

Russell, J. (1987) *Creative Dance in the Primary School*, Northcote House Press, Plymouth.

Report of a Commission of Enquiry (1987) 'Physical Education in Schools', The Physical Education Association of Great Britain and Northern Ireland, London.

Some useful addresses

The Laban Centre for Movement and Dance,
Goldsmith's College, New Cross,
London, SE6 NW.

The Laban Guild,
Sec. Dr. V. Bruce,
Corner Cottage, Skeffington,
Leics. LE7 9YB.

Dance and the Child International,
Sec. G. Williams,
Roehampton Institute of Higher Education,
Roehampton Lane,
London SW15 5PJ.

The National Resource Centre for Dance,
Research officer Judith Chapman,
The University of Surrey,
Guildford, Surrey GU2 5XH.

Movement & Dance Liaison Offices

Northern region
Aykley Heads
DURHAM 5UU
Tel: 0385 49595

North West region
Astley House
Quay Street
MANCHESTER M3 4AE
Tel: 061 834 0338

Yorkshire and Humberside region
Coronet House
Queen Street
LEEDS LS1 4PW
Tel: 0532 436443

East Midlands region
26 Musters Road
West Bridgford
NOTTINGHAM NG2 7PL
Tel: 0602 821887/822586

West Midlands region
Metropolitan House
1 Hagley Road
Five Ways
BIRMINGHAM B16 8TT
Tel: 021 454 3808/9

Eastern region
26–28 Bromham Road
BEDFORD MK40 2QD
Tel: 0234 45222

Greater London & South East region
P O Box 480
Crystal Palace National Sports Centre
Ledrington Road
LONDON SE19 2BQ
Tel: 01 778 8600

Southern region
51A Church Street
Caversham
READING
Berkshire RG4 8AX
Tel: 0734 483311

South West region
Ashlands House
Ashlands
CREWKERNE
Somerset TA18 7LO
Tel: 0460 73491

Index